The Marriage Planner

Planning for every day *after* your Wedding Day

by Robert and Sara Williamson-Bynoe

PRESS

The Marriage Planner
by Robert and Sara Williamson-Bynoe

Printed in the United States of America
ISBN 978-1-60791-531-7

All scenarios are fictional except personal anecdotes told about the authors.

Author Photo: Lambert Francis

www.xulonpress.com

Dedicated to our mothers Dianne and Glenora for giving us life and nurture and to our fathers Bill and George for giving us purpose and identity.

Table of Contents

Acknowledgements

W e wish to express our deepest thanks for the love, friendship and support of Craig and Viviane McLean. We also wish to thank all our friends and family who have been praying for us and who have provided encouragement in this time as we have now come to the end of a very long journey. We would especially like to thank Nigel and Camille Gray for their perseverance in prayer and obedience to the leading of the Holy Spirit in everything. We wish to express our love and appreciation to Edwin and Marsha St. Cyr with whom we now share a spiritual family. Immeasurable thanks to Shari Williamson; having you edit our book has been an immense honor and a blessing. Many others have banded together to pray and to share with others our heart for young couples - we appreciate you immensely. Thank you to all the couples and singles who have eaten at our table, shared their lives, and allowed us to be students of their experiences. Others will be blessed because of what you have imparted to us.

In Him,

Robb and Sara

Prepare **to be Married**

This is truly an exciting time of life. There is something glorious about two lives becoming one. There is so much preparation that goes into the event of a lifetime – your marriage. The very fact that you have chosen to include reading this book as part of your marriage preparation speaks volumes about how seriously you take the Vow you are about to make. Marriage is the "next step" in many peoples' lives once they get to a certain age, or have dated for 2.5 years (as is typically the case), or have completed their education or have finally landed that much sought after job. For the last four years while working on this book we have mused about the "next step" and the preparation it requires.

Are you prepared?

We took it like many of you when we reached one or more of these milestones in our lives. But were we prepared? Well if you had asked us, the timing was right. Our post-secondary education was nearly behind us and we were exploring different career opportunities. We were on our way. But back to the question though, were we prepared for marriage? Well let's see, we did pre-marital counseling with a wonderful pastor and his wife. We talked about different issues from both of our families during our counseling, and we shared a common love for the Lord. Our goals, values, beliefs were all in line with one another. Above all we were friends who loved each other fiercely. But were we *prepared* for *marriage*? Well…no. We had a disaster of a first year. There were fireworks every night in our 300 square foot apartment, and we don't mean the good kind. There were a lot of tears and harsh words and growing pains.

Two people becoming one is hard work. It certainly was for us and for everyone we have talked to who is willing to be honest with us. As we have delved into the mysteries of marriage with many couples over the years, they all say the very same thing — marriage is hard work.

Is being married really that much work?

Now we had heard this phrase tossed around quite a bit that "marriage is hard work." And we even accepted that it *could* be true, but more in a general sense, not as it would relate to *our* marriage. What we did not understand fully is what we now wish to share with you. We did not understand the mechanics of marriage. For us it was similar to driving a car. We had the ability to operate a car but knew little about how to maintain the car or how the car went from being stationary to moving. There were mechanics involved. We were somewhat naïve like many other newlywed couples we have interviewed over the years. We thought that the ability to drive made us experts about our automobile. What we have found is that in addition to the mechanics of operating a vehicle, there is a lot of maintenance that goes along with the freedom and independence that goes with driving a car.

So is marriage like a car? Well, sort of for the sake of this analogy. In order for any relationship to flourish, there are mechanics that need to be understood and applied. Mechanics of course is all about how things work. So we would like to present our ideas about what allows marriage not only to work but to flourish.

Also we talked about maintenance. We all know our cars need oil changes, gasoline and regular maintenance checks in order to keep them on the road. This is the same for your marriage. For example, daily prayer is the fuel that will enable your relationship to grow deeper and stronger. Without consistent prayer a couple will be constantly running on fumes. Marriage requires us to meet each day ready to work, but we can only be rejuvenated by the Holy Spirit for this awesome task.

So why are we writing to you? It is because we wish to celebrate with you in this sacred time. God saw fit for you not to be alone. He cares so much for you. This book was written to equip you with some of the tools we learned over the years. We hope to steer you in the right direction in terms of the really important conversations to have (mechanics), the important values to share (maintenance), and also introduce the keys to a successful thriving marriage. We love marriage. We love that God felt that it was not good for man to be alone and that He created woman as his constant companion. Marriage is beautiful. With preparation, prayers and a lot of love marriage is indeed the event of a lifetime. So come along this journey with us and allow us to be your Marriage Planners.

Chapter *One*

The Vow

*When a man makes a vow to the Lord or takes an
oath to obligate himself by a pledge, he must not
break his word but must do everything he said.*
Numbers 30:3

As we stood hand-in-hand, eyes locked on each other, we heard our pastor's voice directing us to repeat the following, "I promise to love, honor and cherish you 'til death do us part." After the cake was cut, the bouquet was tossed and the caterer was paid, we were left to put these three promises into practice. What is this Vow that we make? Why do we make a Vow and why do we promise our beloved to do these *specific* things?

To answer the first question, the marriage vow that we make is a *covenant*. We see in Scripture that a covenant is the conditional promises made to people by God. The first covenant established on earth was established by God between Himself and humans. But as our definition indicates, this covenant was conditional. The condition of the covenant between man and God was simply obedience. God would be faithful to His Word but humanity must obey His commands. After God had established His covenant with man, He established a covenant between man and woman, that being marriage. Adam sealed the covenant with his wife Eve by calling her "bone of my bones and flesh of my flesh" (Genesis 2:23). They would now be forever unified. As with the covenant between God and man, the covenant between woman and man was conditional. In modern day traditional marriage vows these 'conditions' so to speak are expressed as a promise to love, honor and cherish one another.

So to answer the second question, it is our belief that we make this Vow in order to express what conditions need to be met as part of the marriage covenant. The Vow tells us what the marital relationship is to look like.

Finally, we make these specific promises because this is the essence of what God established in Eden. God intended for man to have love and companionship so He fashioned a wife for Adam. Before woman was created, God assigned man the role of attending to creation. God felt that this was not a task man should do alone, so He assigned woman to come alongside man and help him in this endeavor. The established order of mutual dependence and careful regard of the others' needs is an integral aspect of honor. Finally, the third condition of cherishing ties the first two conditions together. To cherish is simply to care for and treat our spouse like a special person. This involves loving them as well as carefully regarding and attending to their unique needs. Clearly, a marriage based on this kind of promise has the makings of a unity that can only be described as bone of my bone and flesh of my flesh. It is complete oneness. This was God's heart and original design for marriage. And it still is today.

Let's turn now and look specifically at each aspect of the Vow that we have spoken for generations. Your understanding of your marriage Vows cannot be overstated. The Bible says this, "blessed is the man who finds wisdom, the man who gains understanding, for she is more profitable than silver and yields better returns than gold" (Proverbs 3:13-14). There is power of life and death in the spoken word. What we declare has eternal significance and this is especially true of marriage. Let's explore what it means to honor your spouse.

Show Honor

We have been married for ten years and we are only now beginning to understand what it really means to honor each other. Although our marriage continued to grow in many ways, it really began to flourish when we learned how to honor each other. John 3:30 tells us that in order for God to have His way in our lives we must decrease so that He can increase. Similarly, as individuals in a marriage, sometimes we need to "get over ourselves" and decrease so that the marriage can increase. In our experience, it has been our own stubbornness and selfishness that blocks the pathway to honor. We can become so concerned about being "right" that we ignore the promise we made to honor our spouse.

Honor is crucial to a marriage. Honor can be expressed as a courteous regard for another. Often times we find it easy to be courteous to perfect strangers but struggle to show regard for our own spouse. Acts of courtesy towards others come quite naturally for most of us. For instance, by opening doors, holding elevators, and taking time to listen to a friend talk about their difficult day, we show courtesy.

Honor by doing the simple things

Honor comes from doing the simple things. A husband honors his wife by, fixing the sink when she asks him to, changing the light bulb that's too high for her to reach and, taking off his shoes when she has just mopped the floor. A wife honors her husband by protecting his vulnerabilities instead of using them against him. For example, if your husband is more of a scholar than a handy-man, focus on his strengths rather than his short comings. The Bible speaks of the tongue as being a two-edged sword. It can uplift or tear someone down. A wife honors her husband by speaking edifying words.

Doing things that show honor brings joy to your spouse. It invites trust. If a wife knows her husband will do what he says he will do, this says to her, "my word is good" and she learns to trust and rely on that. When a husband knows he is safe to be vulnerable with his wife, this translates, "I can trust you with my heart. I can show up. I can be me. I can ask for what I need without fear of rejection." To honor is powerful.

Being honored is your spouse's deep desire

In talking to couples married for one year and those married for thirty years, it becomes clear that a common desire is to be honored. Men often complain about being nagged. However, it is important to understand that nagging is a by-product of a woman feeling dishonored. Nagging does not work, but it takes place just before a wife closes a chamber of her heart off to her husband. It is like a last ditch effort to have her needs met. Generally, husbands do not respond well to nagging...no one does! However, a wise husband will take a moment to ask, "What does she really need from me?" Often your wife is asking for your God given strength. She has a need that requires your assistance and in some cases, your strength, whether physical or emotional. She will keep asking until that need is met or until she comes to accept that her need will not be met and that asking for your help will do her no good. If husbands can hear a wife's request as simply a need that requires attention and then attend to that need as soon as possible, it eliminates nagging and invites security and trust. We will examine this point further in upcoming chapters.

On the flip side, women often complain that their husbands "do not open up." They feel that although they do their best to communicate their own needs, their husbands leave them in the dark when it comes to his needs. As an honoring wife, it is important to remember that speaking encouraging words is the key to opening up and maintaining healthy communication. A spouse who feels dishonored will not open up. If your husband seems closed off when you get into a discussion, be sensitive to why that may be. Many husbands have been exposed to the nagging-then-shut down dance between a man and a woman as they were growing up. This dance may have already begun in your own relationship, but if you have done the dance you have already experienced that it just does not work. Requests for honor are usually simple. "Please put your clothes away, please stick to this week's budget, and please speak to me with respect."

The exchange between a husband and a wife becomes simple the more each is honored. The difficulty comes because it is against our nature to be honoring, we leave our clothes lying around, we overspend by buying those shoes because after all we deserve it, we yell…you get the picture. We are constantly fighting the tendency to be stubborn and selfish yet what we all deeply desire is to be cared for with courteous regard. Remember, what you want is also what your spouse wants, but it must start with you. Resist the flesh the Bible tells us, show honor.

Cherish Me

Do we even know what the word *cherish* means anymore? It seems like one of those words that has gone out of style like "reckon" or "henceforth". When we think about things that we cherish, sentimental possessions come to mind. Possessions like a Babe Ruth rookie card or a precious pearl necklace passed down through several generations. The word cherish is also used when we think of special memories or experiences that have shaped us into who we are today. However, is cherish a word that comes to mind when we consider how we regard our spouse? If we were playing Scategories and *cherish* was the category that the game was asking for to describe how we treat our partner, I think most of us would still be grasping for the answer long after the buzzer sounded. Yet, while hundreds stood in witness, you promised to *cherish* each other until you breathed your last.

A cherished spouse is a well-spring of joy

To cherish your spouse is to esteem her and take immense pleasure in her. When we realized that we were not really cherishing each other two thoughts came to mind. The first thought frankly was, "Oh great, here's something else that we should be doing but we aren't doing". The second thought was, "Okay what do we have to do to cherish each other?" Well let's go back to the examples that we cited earlier. Let's start with the invaluable baseball card. We would probably have it enclosed in one of those clear plastic cases to make sure it did not get creased or damaged by the oils of human hands. As for the set of pearls, we would probably keep them locked away in a special jewelry box. These pearls would only be worn on special occasions or taken out for a good polishing. Now before we get ahead of ourselves, we are not saying that we should stow our loved one away in a case or a box, only to look at them now and then. What we are saying is that we show each other that we are cherished by the way we treat one another day to day. As husbands, we need to get away from showering our wives with compliments because we expect something in return. It is important to let your wife know that she is a beautiful treasure all of the time. As wives, we cannot take for granted the things that our husbands do for us. Although he may have only completed 5 of the 10 things on the honey-do list, we need to praise him for the 5 completed tasks before we "remind" him about the 5 incomplete ones. A man simply thrives under the praises of his trea-sured wife. He will do more to please you because he feels so appreciated.

By showing your spouse that he is cherished, we have seen that this produces lasting joy in a relation-ship. If we focus more on cherishing each other and less time highlighting short comings, the whole tone of our relationship will be more joyous. Now when you first get started you may feel like a salmon swimming upstream against the current. As is the case of showing honor, when this becomes an integral part of how you relate to each other you will not want to stop.

Love Never Fails

I recall nearing the end of our pre-marital coun-seling. I asked our pastor's wife, "Why do I need to love Robert? I know the Lord has chosen him for me."

She simply said, "Love gets you through the hard times." That is the one thing I have remembered and that holds absolutely true. When we enter into marriage with the one the Lord has chosen for us, that entering in is an act of obedience. However, that obedience is not what sustains a couple through the difficult times. It is Love. Now that we have established the value of love, how do we live it out day to day?

Hollywood has offered us countless examples of romantic love; *You've Got Mail, Jerry McGuire, The Notebook* and *Titanic* to name a few. What are some notable commonalities with these movies? Guy meets girl, and whether in an instant or over a period of time, a mutual bond of attraction forms. This bond could be driven by physical attraction, a natural chemistry, or for some other reasons. As time goes on, a relationship develops, feelings grow stronger and eventually, the "L" word begins to be tossed around. But what is love? The Bible tells us that,

> Love...is patient, love is kind, it does not envy, it does not boast, it is not proud. It is not rude, it is not self-seeking, it is not easily angered, it keeps no record of wrong. Love does not delight in evil, but rejoices with the truth. It always protects, always trusts, always hopes, always perseveres, love never fails...and now these three remain faith, hope and love. But the greatest of these is love (1Corinthians 13:4-6).

The ability to love is supernatural

Wow, that is a tall order! It can be difficult to keep this all in perspective. But now let us contrast

23

this biblical description of love with the Hollywood portrayal of love. If we were to apply these attributes of love to the couples in the movies, would we really think they love each other? I'm certain that if you decided to rent all these flicks again and review them with the biblical "love checklist" in hand, you would probably find that some of these characteristics of love are present, but not all. In order for all of these elements of love to be present, there would have to be some sort of supernatural presence. The presence would have to be God. Because God is the very embodiment of love, we just can't love on our own strength. We might be able to pull off some of the qualities sometimes, but not all of them all the time. If we follow God's divine providence, at least we have a winning chance. After all, God is love.

Unfortunately, we see many Christians and certainly folks in secular society taking their cues from Hollywood about how their relationships ought to function. Time and time again our best effects are met with failure and we ask why. We fail to truly love in *our* own strength because love is a supernatural phenomenon. It is God at work in and through us. Only He can teach us how to love and there is no hope to love and be loved outside of his divine operation.

When we talk about *God's* love we aren't talking about religion. Religion does not love anyone, and it cannot teach anyone how to love. It is merely a social construct of man and for many people an idol that is worshipped. God's love leads us into a relationship with the Creator of the heavens and this earth, as well as with one another. We come into relationship with God through His Son Jesus. And Jesus teaches us how to love. Marriage is not a relationship of two it is a relationship of three. With God as the centre of your marriage, and as you pray each day with your spouse, He will teach you not only how to love your spouse, but also, the mysteries of marriage.

Chapter *Two*

Twenty Questions to ask before your Vows

Search me, O God, and know my heart;
test me and know my anxious thoughts.
Psalm 139:23

What if there were twenty questions you could ask your partner before you got married which could tell you whether you marriage will last or end in divorce? Would you ask the questions? Most people would say, "Yes absolutely, I would want to know ahead of time, I want a guarantee!" Although we are not offering guarantees, we are offering twenty questions that will give you important indicators of where your future marriage is headed. The rest is up to you, your partner and the Lord.

The questions that we are going to ask and answer are divided into five sections. The first is motive. Our goal is to have you as a couple explore your motives for getting married. We seek to have compatible couples succeed in marriage, however it is also our goal to have some of you discover whether you and your partner are incompatible for marriage and walk away *before* the Vows. Clearly if you are engaged to be married you are committed to and love your partner. Well…maybe not. We have seen time and again in the church and outside of the church where couples get married for all the wrong reasons. This is why it is so important to explore your motives to make sure they are right.

Next we will look at expectations. In relationships, whether we are aware of it or not, we hold certain expectations of others. While expectations can be harmful, this side of heaven, we probably will not do away with them all together. The reason expectations can be harmful is because they invite others to perform to our satisfaction. That can be difficult for people to do for us. We all know how difficult it is for us to do this for others. At some point we will disappoint the other person, even when we are trying to do our very best – for some people your very best may not be enough. So in marriage you can see that having certain expectations and requiring that they be met by our spouse is problematic at best. We all fail, disappoint and fall short at times. Holding set-in-stone expectations can lead to hurt and resentment in marriage because no one can perform at his or her very best at all times. A more helpful approach is to live with anticipation. We will talk about this more later.

When you began to fall in love with your spouse there was a feeling of anticipation to see him or to hear from her. There was a yearning for this person. Now these romantic feelings temper with time but the anticipation can remain forever. Rather than expecting her to make a big turkey dinner like *your* mom did, anticipate your first Christmas together and all the new traditions you will be able to create together.

We also explore the process of becoming a couple. There is a process or a journey with everything in life. As we write this, we're watching our four year old put together a puzzle for the first time. She has pieces from two different puzzles and is trying to place different pieces together to see which ones fit. She has a method that she needs to execute before she gets to enjoy the finished product. Marriage is like this. There is a process of coming together. There is trial and error. Some pieces may not fit and will have to be placed elsewhere, while others may have to be done away with. The end result is a picture of beauty that glorifies God.

The next group of questions look at outlook. How we see our circumstance is very telling about how we will move through it. A bright outlook will color how we meet the challenges and triumphs that come in our marital relationship. Whether we are able to have a bright outlook often times has to do with what we experienced growing up. If we saw a healthy and happy marriage between our mom and dad we too will see marriage as a healthy and happy union, and will work to establish and maintain it as such. However, if we saw a lot of dysfunction and unhappiness, we may struggle to see how marriage can be any other way. The legacy that we are left by our parents is a factor in how we lay the foundation of our own marital union. We may determine to never do the things that we saw our parents do, or we may want to emulate what we saw. Whatever your position, our family of origin plays a role in what our marriage will be. While we may have an intimate understanding of our own experience with marriage, we may not be as aware of our partner's experience. It is important to know this because it will have a direct influence on your spouse's behaviour, especially during difficult times. Asking outlook questions is literally attempting to understand *where* your spouse is coming from.

Finally we ask you what we call providence questions. That is, what God's role or function is in marriage in general and your relationship specifically. It is also critical to look at your personal relationship with God. We know that without Christ at the centre of your marriage it cannot be all that it is intended to be. Many marriages survive without God, but we are not talking about mere survival. We hope to see marriages thrive and flourish. Such marriages produce godly offspring that will shape and change our world and advance God's kingdom. In our experience, growing your marriage with God's help is kingdom work.

So let's get started. We have not only asked, but answered these questions to help as a guide. Your answers will be unique of course, because they are to be personal, based on your own experiences. We encourage you to work separately through the questions once you have finished the book. After you have completed your answers, come back together and discuss the questions and each of your answers. Let's begin the journey.

Chapter *Three*

Motives

Now a man named Ananias, together with his wife Sapphira, also sold a piece of property. With his wife's full knowledge he kept back part of the money for himself, but brought the rest and put it at the apostles' feet. Acts 5:1-2

Here we see in Acts 5:1&2 that the motive of Ananias' and Sapphira's hearts to withhold some of the money intended for the advancement of the gospel was exposed. They knew that all the profits from the sale of their land should be brought to the apostles. Because of their deception they both died when they brought only a portion of their profit to the Lord. We encourage couples not to withhold the motives of *their* hearts before their marriage. The truth will always lead to life.

Question One

Why do you want to get married?

As the world continues to pull further and further

away from tradition, we can't help but ask this question. As we fall away from the structure of the life of yesterday, a high percentage of singles we have had opportunity to talk with still would marry. But what is the attraction to this union of commitment in a world afraid to commit? What about the negative depiction of marriage in the media? As the next generation is taught the dos and don'ts of marriage from Hollywood, how could they possibly want any part of it? After watching failed marriage after failed marriage in the entertainment industry many still find themselves drawn to the idea of married life. There is a paradox here.

However the reason so many people are drawn to marriage goes back to the creation of man. It was not long after man was created before God identified the need for man to have companionship as He said it was not good for man to be alone. God gives Adam Eve to complete the picture of creation. It is engrained in our DNA to desire the companionship of the opposite sex. As God completed Adam by uniting him to Eve, we today are completed when we submit ourselves to a Holy covenant of marriage under God. Although we believe that God has chosen individuals to remain single, we also believe that he would have many of us to marry.

On a personal level begin to think about the reasons you wish to marry *your* partner. Many people have a pull toward marriage. You are obviously among that number, however search your heart and seek God to reveal your motives for entering this commitment.

Question Two

Why don't you want to be single?

This question is a spin off from the previous one. Although the questions sound similar, there are some differences. There has always seemed to be a negative stigma associated with being single particularly among Christians. A girl who is thirty and single is looked upon with pity. A single guy in his forties is seen as having a clear deficiency in his life. You need only watch a half-hour of primetime television and you can see how *cool* it is to be in a relationship and how *not cool* it is to be single. On the issue of singleness the church and the world seem to be in agreement. The message in the media and even at times in the church unfortunately, is not the idea of being in a quality, meaningful relationship. The message is, "It doesn't really matter who you're with, just don't be alone." We want couples to understand that lives can be ruined when you choose to marry the wrong person rather than stay single.

By doing this we create *Ishmaels* before we are able to receive our *Isaac*. If only we could have a quantum leap experience into the future to see the destruction that comes along with "just dating anyone." The devastation of surrendering your heart to the girl with the pretty smile or the guy with the cool car can leave scarring effects.

God did not bring man and woman together just to fulfil our sexual desires and give us social status. He created a union based on love, honor, respect and self-sacrifice. If we seek companionship with these characteristics, we will experience the joy that comes with such a relationship. But if our goal is simply not to be single, you are setting yourself up for potential heartbreak. We have all been single and understand how unpleasant it can be at times. However, it does not compare to the pain associated with being in a relationship that had no future before it began. We think Adam took the best approach when it came to taking a mate – he waited for God to bring him one.

Chapter *Four*

Expectations

My soul, wait silently for God alone,
for my expectation is from Him.
Psalm 62:5(NKJV)

The world offers us many ideas of what we can expect from marriage. However, we are told in Psalm 62:5 that our expectation must come from God. We talked in an earlier chapter about living in a state of anticipation rather than expectation. When we anticipate our life with our partner, there is a sense of hopefulness that goes with it. As we discuss your expectations here, we hope to get you thinking about what you actually envision your married life to be, while bearing in mind that our expectations will come from God as we wait on Him.

Question Three

What expectations do you have about being married?

Whenever we set out to accomplish a goal, we

have a general idea of what awaits us at the finish line. When someone says, "I have a goal that I would like to see become a reality", a typical follow up question is, "Well, what does your goal look like?" The question is asking about his vision – that is, how he expects to meet his goal. When an entrepreneur goes to a bank to apply for a business loan to open his coffeehouse, the bank will want to see a business plan. This business plan will outline the entrepreneur's expectations leading to his success. In his plan he will look at details like a marketing analysis summary, strategy and implementation, keys to success and a financial plan. He can't simply say that his coffee and pastries taste great and expect the bank to cut him a check and send him on his way. He must satisfy the bank's expectations by clearly outlining his vision.

Likewise, when a couple feels that they are ready to get married, they must first have a vision for their marriage. They shouldn't simply spend all of their time and energy planning their wedding day. They will also need to invest a significant amount of time planning what their actual marriage will look like. It is very seldom that we pause and think, "If we have to put all this time into planning the first day of marriage, how much *more* time should we put into planning the rest our lives together." If more couples would adopt this mindset, we would see a significant decline in the divorce rate in the church and in North America as a whole. This being said, it is crucial for couples to have a firm idea of expectations when it comes to marriage. We can't expect a marriage to succeed when we don't take time to assess what our expectations are. There is an expression that says, if we fail to plan, we plan to fail.

Hundreds of coffeehouses come and go every year in North America. Although there numerous reasons to explain their demise, lack of planning and failure to set a clear vision play significant roles. The same can be said about marriages. We ask you this question about expectations because many people are not aware that they have expectations of being married. Others are not clear about what their expectations are. They know what they don't want when faced with a situation that displeases them, but they did not give their personal hopes, dreams, fears, and desires a voice prior to their nuptials. It can be very disillusioning for young couples to stumble upon one another's expectations accidentally.

Take Jake and his wife Denise. Denise often dreamed of her wedding night because she would finally be able try to conceive a baby with Jake whom she had been courting for two years. She loved everything about Jake and was excited about starting a family right away. Jake and Denise had decided to save their first kiss for their wedding day and as the day drew near Denise's anticipation built. Jake was completely smitten with Denise. He had loved her from the moment he laid eyes on her at youth camp and their romance was everything he had hoped for and more. He was excited about travelling overseas with Denise as a couple and perhaps doing some short-term mission work with a few other couples they knew. They had always talked about doing this. He too was looking forward to their wedding day and night.

Even though this well-intentioned couple had shared many of their dreams with one another, their dream of a baby versus international travel was not thoroughly discussed. It quite frankly was a point of tension that both of them found to be unpleasant. They were at least in agreement about travelling and mission work, but what about a baby? Denise expected Jake to come around and Jake expected Denise to give them some time to be a couple before they assumed the responsibility of a family; after all there would be plenty of time.

This is very common. For some couples they are aware of their issues that produce unwanted tension, others are caught off guard. It is critical not carry unresolved issues especially around expectations into your marriage. The pain this can cause is simply not worth putting off the serious heart to heart talks you need to have while you are still engaged. Talking heart to heart, transparently and honestly will also reveal expectations you did not know each of you has.

Question Four

What does the ideal marriage look like?

When we think of the ideal marriage, what is the first image that pops into our heads? For many it is the wedding day. The Bride is wearing the latest creation from a well known designer, complete with flawless make-up and hair that is all accented by a perpetually radiant smile. While the groom, miraculously transforms into Brad Pitt in an Armani suit. But what about after the cake is cut, the guests have gone home and the plane hits the tarmac returning from that sunny destination? What next? Now that we've had a chance to ponder it for a moment, we see that quite a bit more thought is required.

First, we must think if we even know what an ideal marriage looks like. Do we know anyone whose has an ideal marriage? What about that of our parents' or grandparents'? What about our friend's parent's marriage or our pastor's marriage. Now that we have begun to think about who might have an ideal marriage, you need to determine what attributes are found in an ideal marriage. This is where you really need to begin to define what marriage looks like. What are some things that you must have in your marriage that would make it ideal? What are some things that you *refuse* to have in your marriage to make it ideal? This is where you need to begin to build a blueprint of your marriage so when it comes time to build it, you will already have your plans in hand. Finally, you must also consider that what may be ideal for the bride may not be ideal for the groom. So be willing to be honest about what your personal ideal is for your marriage and be open to hearing what your partner has to share.

Question Five

What don't you want in a marriage?

Unfortunately, this is one of the questions that couples come up with an answer to *after* the "I dos". Perhaps one of the most commonly uttered phrases that newly married couples use in an argument is, "If I only knew that about you!" The unfortunate reality is that most couples don't put enough thought into what they don't want in a marriage. As for those few who take the time to think about it, sometimes they will compromise and lower their standards. In doing so, they try to accept what they don't want in a marriage with the hope that what they *are* getting will be a reasonable payoff. If you will keep those "don't wants" at the forefront of your minds instead of allowing them to slip into the background, they will help to save you from a lot of grief.

Many people hope that they do not need to address issues that may potentially create tension. The belief is that these issues will somehow work themselves out throughout the course of the marriage. Most couples will attest that the changes that were expected in their new spouse did not happen after marriage. In our opinion, sticking to your guns where "don't wants" are concerned is critical to the success of a marriage. For instance, Steve is an avid hockey fan. When Kayla visits his apartment for the first time, she notices that every inch of his place is adorned with sports memorabilia. Without discussing it with Steve, Kayla expects that when they move into their home after the wedding day, most of Steve's things will find their way into a box in the garage. As far as Steve is concerned, his collection will take its rightful place in the living room. Although this is a light-hearted example, many couples enter marriage with far more serious "don't wants" that they fail to discuss. Before long, these issues begin to erode the susceptible foundation of the marriage.

Marriage is challenging enough when you are on the same page about most issues. It will prove to be even more difficult when you find yourself living with something that you did not want in your marriage in the first place. It will eat away at the life of your marriage like a malignancy, increasing the chance of you becoming a divorce statistic. Two exercises that we strongly recommend are as follows:

1. Write down absolutely everything that you do not want in your marriage and place them in order of importance.
2. Discuss with your partner any scenarios that you can think of to get an idea about how you really feel about different issues. Questions like, *"What would you do if..."* or *"How would you react if..."* are insightful. Not only will these exercises help you get to know each other better, they will help you to prepare for issues as they arise.

NOTE: Please be aware that these exercises will be fun for the girls but painful for the guys. With that being said, they will prove to be another great way to help establish a strong foundation for your marriage.

Question Six

What do you think you could bring to a marriage?

Enough thought often isn't given to what *you* have to offer in marriage. We seldom ask ourselves, "What attributes will *I* bring to my marriage that I feel would lead to its success? Again, here is a question that is meant to get you thinking and to make sure all the bases are covered before you're "equally yoked". Here are a few ideas to get you thinking.

When an athlete decides to try out for a sports team, there are a number of steps that lead to his attending tryouts. To begin with, at some stage it was discovered that the athlete has certain natural abilities that excels her past what would be considered average. After this realization, the athlete would have to devote time to honing and developing these skills. After strengthening a sound understanding and skill set for the sport, the athlete needs to cater her game to play a certain style or position. Again, this will lean heavily on her natural gifting and developed set of skills. For example in the game of basketball, if a player is 6 feet 5 inches tall, can handle the ball well and has a good three point shot, he has the makings of a point guard. In football, if a player is 6 feet 4 inches tall, weighs 260 pounds and is quick on his feet, he would make a good Linebacker. In order for these athletes to be successful in their respective sports, they need to develop an intimate understanding of what the sport is all about. Once they've done this, they begin an intensive and sacrificial journey toward mastering the sport. This is the type of approach that couples need to take when they are contemplating what they can bring to a marriage.

Individually, each of you must consider your personal strengths and weaknesses. In doing so, you will begin to see what areas need refining both as individuals and as a couple.

Question Seven

What do you want your partner to bring to your marriage?

Now that you've thought about what you can bring to a marriage, you can now start to think about what you want your partner to contribute to the marriage. Let us first begin by saying that this is an area that you want to have some specific ideas in mind. Many people who have been through a divorce will tell you that if they had invested more time in this exercise, their lives would be different today. Our humble opinion is that people are so terrified of ending up alone, that they are not honest with them-selves or their partner when it comes to expectations. We believe it is better to be alone before marriage than to be alone after a divorce. If you are truly committed to the idea that marriage is a *"till death do us part"* commitment, then you *must* have a good sense of who it is that you are marrying. If both part-ners are taking this approach, then you will be laying a strong foundation for a good marriage plan. As was suggested earlier in the chapter, come up with a list that fully describes what you want in a partner. You may find that your partner gets some Xs along with those check marks. However, you will be that much further ahead than if you had kept your expectations to yourself.

Question eight

Define your ideal spouse.

Now that you have an idea of what you want your spouse to bring to your marriage, you can give some thought towards your *ideal* spouse. Now this may seem like a repeat of the previous question, however this question refers more to personality characteristics. It's easy to say that you are looking for someone who is smart, good looking and funny…well who isn't. The idea of this chapter is to think of what you imagine your spouse to be like. Now we could generalize and say, "Orlando Bloom or Jennifer Lopez would be my ideal spouse." But we don't really know them. Sure Orlando is handsome and funny but that doesn't tell us anything about his personality. Yes, JLo is attractive and talented, but those attributes don't speak to her character. To begin writing down what we would consider to be ideal in a spouse, we must first look introspectively so we have a solid understanding of our own personality characteristics.

Is it realistic to say you're looking for a partner who is physically active when the only physical activity you get is getting your snack back into the TV room before the commercial break is over? Or is it realistic to say that you're looking for someone who has a heart for advancing God's kingdom, when you are concerned only with *yours*? Personally reflecting what it is you are seeking in a spouse goes a long way in attracting that person to you.

Question nine

Define what your ideal spouse is not.

While working on the previous question, you may be answering this question at the same time. There is hardly a better way to find what you are looking for than when you are confronted with what you *don't* want. This question may also be accompanied with a piece of humble pie if you realize that you possess some of the qualities that you don't want in a spouse. You may also find when you are half way through your list you wouldn't want to marry yourself. That's okay; this realization presents an opportunity for growth and self-improvement. A man who is led towards a woman who is tender and compassionate may not have these characteristics himself; therefore he will need to develop in these areas in order to attract her. Similarly, a woman who does not want a man who is financially irresponsible should exhibit good financial stewardship. We encourage you to be thorough yet realistic when considering what you do not want in a spouse. This exercise is not intended for you to find the perfect spouse, but an *ideal* one for you.

Question ten

How much of you would you like to see in your partner?

Here is a question that may have been partially answered by completing the two preceding questions. Are there any characteristics that you possess that you would like your partner to possess? Again, there are some obvious answers here but let's unpack this some more. If you are known as the funny one in the crowd, would you like to be with someone who is as funny as you? Or if you are passionate about education would you like for your spouse to have a similar passion? As we conclude this section of the questionnaire, we hope that your expectations have become deeper and more defined. As is the case with any of life's major decisions, you must look at everything from all angles to be able to make the best decision.

Chapter *Five*

Process

So it came to pass in the process of time that
Hannah conceived and bore a son, and called his
name Samuel, saying, "Because I have asked
for him from the LORD."
1 Samuel 1:20 (NKJV)

Here we have Hannah, a woman with a longing in her heart for a son. There was nothing she could do in her own strength to bring about her desires. But she did something that we have done in our own lives and we encourage you to do as well. She sought the Lord and put her need before him. As we see, the Lord answered her prayers and Hannah responded by naming her son Samuel, to reflect that God acknowledged and answered the longing of her heart. Likewise, the process of finding a spouse must include seeking and then waiting on God to answer.

Question Eleven

How would you go about finding your spouse?

Now that you have solidified what it is that you're

looking for in a life partner, you can focus your energies on going about finding him or her. So where do you begin? Let's just brainstorm for a moment about where to meet a mate. Bearing in mind that searching for a mate is a social exercise, we would probably be led to places where social activities take place like parties, sporting events, weddings or professional development events. Because these are places where people put forth their best image, it would seem to be an ideal place to find that "special someone". But, how many times have we met someone at one of these social gatherings and found out later that they are not who they say they are?

This is what we call putting on a social mask. A social mask is what someone uses to hide his shortcomings by pretending to be what he is not. In a way, he is recreating himself to fool others into believing he is someone he isn't. We are not simply talking about a girl who wears too much make-up or a guy who says he has a high profile job when he actually works at the mall. We are talking about individuals who are trying to get the "big ones" passed you. For instance, trying to convince you that they're well-off, well educated, or that they will start coming out to church once you are married. A suitor may even say that he has a personal relationship with the Lord when his lifestyle tells you otherwise.

We have said all of that to ask you this. What is the best approach to finding a partner who you would like to spend the rest of your life with? What approach do you take when making any other of life's big decisions? Would you take a superficial or careless approach to choosing a major in college, buying a car or buying a house? Of course not! You would take your time and do your research to make sure that you are making a decision that is best for you.

This is also the approach that you must take if you are planning to find your ideal mate. If you are looking for a person that is well educated, you will look for them in college (but *not* at a fraternity "kegger"). If you are looking for someone who shares your dedication to your faith, you will look for that ideal mate at a house of worship. If you are affiliated with a certain political organization, you will look for that individual at related gatherings. The bottom line is this, if you are purposely looking for someone specific, you can't hope to find them accidentally. The most important thing to remember is that you are looking for the mate that God has for you. When you approach it this way, it will help to you think of places where you should be spending your time.

Question Twelve

How would you draw this person to you?

This question requires a good dose of introspection and honesty. Now that you have a good idea of what it is you are looking for in a mate, you need to ask yourself a couple of questions.

Ask yourself, "If I met the right person at the right place at the right time and he/she is all that I could ever imagine and more, would they be attracted to me?"

The next question that you should ask yourself is, "When I meet someone I'm interested in, am I wearing a social mask?"

These are questions that require you to be *real* about the process of finding your life partner. Although it is an expression that we are not big fans of, "you are what you eat" seems to fit well here. In our experience, one of the best examples of this deals with your devotion to your faith. We have heard countless stories of individuals who are looking for a mate who has a committed relationship with Jesus Christ yet do not have a strong Christian walk. An individual who takes an active role in his church, tithes consistently and is an upstanding citizen in his community will be looking for the same qualities in a spouse. However, if you pray only when you want something, go to church twice a year and would rather take money out of the offering plate than put money in, you likely will not attract the godly spouse you seek. So with this in mind, you must have a true picture of who you are as this will give you a good indication of who you will attract.

Chapter *Six*

Outlook

...And live a life of love, just as Christ loved us and gave himself up for us as a fragrant offering and sacrifice to God. Ephesians 5:2

The next group of questions are to help you explore what your outlook on marriage is. By outlook we mean the way you view marriage. This view often comes to us from what we have experienced of marriage in our lives. The marriage of our parents and those who are close to us has the greatest influence on us. The way we view marriage is also very telling about how we see ourselves. Do we feel we have a lot to offer a spouse, or do we need a partner to enhance us because we feel we are deficient in some way? The Bible gives us the best outlook to take when it comes to marriage. We are to live a life of love, because this is how Jesus showed us how to live. Our goal should always be to love as Christ loved.

Question Thirteen

What does being married mean to you?

This question is not asking for *your* definition of marriage. It is asking you what role you see marriage playing in your life overall. Not only does addressing this question give you a better understanding of yourself, it will also give you an understanding of how your future spouse sees marriage as well. For women, usually there are strong emotions tied to marriage. The idea of having someone to love and protect them is a significant aspect of marriage. For men, there is a certain level of pride attached to being married. He can now hold his head up high and say, "I got my woman", as if he were Tiger Woods putting on his Master's green jacket in the clubhouse. Also, to a man marriage means having someone to care for who respects and appreciates him in a way that only a woman can.

It is an unfortunate reality, but for some, they think about how "long" their marriage will last. In today's society, it has become increasingly common to place a timeline on your marriage. This idea may be in your partner's head because they are a product of divorce. They may not be able to imagine being married forever, because his or her parents were divorced by the time they were eight years old. There may also be commitment issues that affect the duration of a marriage. You might find out that your partner's commitment issues will have a negative affect on your marriage. She may put forth the same commitment to the marriage that she has to other commitments she's broken. Perhaps there is a college degree that your partner has been promising to go back and finish for the past five years, or maybe he has trouble keeping a job for longer than six months. These are but a couple of examples of broken commitments. Depending on how a person is influenced, there can be many other factors that lend to his definition of marriage. It is for this reason that we strongly urge you to answer these questions honestly and independently, to ensure you come up with the most truthful answers. It is better to be painfully honest now than to go through the pain of divorce later.

Question Fourteen

How much of you do you see in your partner?

If you were honest in answering question 10, you may very well have a lump in your throat right now. But that's okay. If nothing else, your objective here is to find out as much about yourself and your partner before you marry. So take the time to ask a lot of questions to explore who your partner is. This will help you to see how similar or different you really are. Although it is good to have some similarities, it is not necessarily the best situation to marry a clone of your self. As we can all admit, there are some things about ourselves that drive *us* nuts. You don't really need to have that duplicated by your partner, now do you? But at the same time, you don't want to have a relationship where your partner is so different from you that you can't come to a consensus on the simplest decisions. It's good to have a good set of commonalities, but it is also good to mix it up so you can keep things fresh and interesting. If she likes more exotic food and you like fast food, trying out what each likes not only adds diversity to the relationship, but allows each person to be celebrated as an individual. By embracing your partner you must embrace how they may be different from you as well.

While there should be things a couple has in common, like a shared faith, it is not essential to marry someone who is just like you. Nor is it healthy to try and change your partner to be more like you. It is important to remember that God created us as unique individuals. Your partner's uniqueness is likely what attracted you to them in first place.

Question Fifteen

How much does your partner complement you?

Now, when we talk about how your partner complements you, we are not talking about how many times he tells you that your hair looks nice. When we speak of how your partner complements you, we are referring to how they enhance your weak areas to make them strong. A good example of this is if Matt is good with finances he can set up a budget with Ana who seems to have holes in her pocket when it comes to money. Another simple example of this is with cooking. Who will be the cook of the house? One of you may love to cook and enjoys cooking for the other. But if neither of you know how to cook, you may want to take cooking classes together. As you get to know each other better through court-ship, more of the puzzle pieces will fall into place. However, to make sure nothing is overlooked, sit down with your mate and begin to talk about your individual strengths and weaknesses. This dialogue will prove to be another opportunity for you to set the blueprint for a strong and lasting marriage.

Chapter *Seven*

Providence

The name of the Lord is a strong tower;
the righteous run to it and are safe.
Proverbs 18:10

These final few questions deal with our own obedience and reliance on God. As Christians we are called to be righteous before our God. In order to be righteous, we must do what is *right* in His eyes. In order for God to reveal His will and providence in our lives, we must first allow him to be the Lord of our lives.

Question Sixteen

What sort of legacy have you been left regarding marriage?

By asking this question, we are looking to unwrap how you have been influenced through the marriages of others. By answering this question, you will examine what experiences have helped you formulate your understanding of what marriage is. This influence has come to be known as a legacy. A legacy is that which is established in one generation and passed on to the next. In the case of marriage, there are legacies established that help in setting up a positive marriage environment for the next generation. On the other hand however, there are legacies that can effectively destroy a marriage before it even gets off the ground. An element of a positive legacy is team parenting. This is a situation where both parents take active roles is rearing their children. Rather than mom having to cook, clean, chauffeur and help out with homework, Dad can drive the kids to Tae Kwan Do after *he* loads the dishwasher. Instead of Dad being forced to be "default disciplinarian", mom can take an equal role in this area as well.

An example of a bad legacy is that of abuse. Whether it is of a physical or emotional nature, abuse plays a profound role in how one understands marriage. If you have been passed down a legacy of abuse for most of your life, this situation becomes *your* normal. However, what you consider normal may be very disarming to your partner. For example, when you and your spouse get into your first super-fight, you might be ready to argue for twelve rounds hoping to get a "knockout" along the way. Your spouse however, may want to retreat to the nearest closet and close the door behind her because she is not used to such loud shouting. It is for this reason this question is so important. What is even more important is having a good understanding of what you have been left with for your marriage legacy. When you and your partner have come up with exhaustive lists of what your legacies are, you can begin to "cut and paste" the good and the bad as you begin to create your own legacy for a healthy marriage.

Question Seventeen

What is God's role in marriage?

Throughout the various questions in this questionnaire, we have touched on what roles could be played by the wife and the husband. But not much has been said about God's role in marriage. For some couples God is an integral component of their marriage. As for others, God's job is completed after the groom is given the green light to kiss the bride. If this is your approach, bear the following in mind. If you are entering an agreement under God's authority, wouldn't it make sense that God's role in the situation would be significant? Say for example you got a call from NBC and the guy on the other end of the phone tells you that he wants to produce that sitcom idea that you are always talking about. Do you think he will hand you the keys to the studio and say, "Let me know what time the show comes on?" Probably not! Since it can be said that God is the Executive Producer of marriage, you can be certain that He wants to have an active role in His "pilot" to make sure it doesn't get taken off the air after the first episode.

Now that we have made a case for God's role in marriage, how does it work in a practical sense?

Well, let's start with prayer, end with prayer and use prayer at every point in between. It's been said that the couple that prays together stays together. The best way to ensure that God gets His input in your marriage is to take all your thanks, cares, praises and concerns to Him. Now as is the case with all prayer, God may not give you the answers that you are looking for. He may not make your wife suddenly interested in watching football every Sunday after church, nor make your husband want to go to the garden store with you instead of golfing with the guys. But what God will do is give you a covering of blessing and protection if you devote your marriage to pleasing Him. In God's eyes, when we marry under His authority we become one flesh. To God, when He looks at a couple, it can be said that he sees only one individual in service to Him. So investigate how others have been blessed by allowing God to guide their marriages. Then make sure that your marriage is open to God's direction. As God tells us in Ecclesiastes 4:2 "...a three fold cord is not easily broken."

Question Eighteen

What does God's Word say about marriage?

As was suggested in question 17, we strongly suggest that you gain a good understanding of what God tells us about marriage. If it is your intention to live a life for God and to submit your life and your marriage to Him, you should have a good idea of what the *play* book says. Look into the relationship that Abraham had with Sarah; that Noah had with his wife, and that Joseph and Mary had. Gain a good understanding of the struggles they had and how God helped them to overcome them. Then, study what the prophets, Jesus Christ and the apostles tell us about marriage. Just as it is important to have personal relationship with Jesus Christ, it is also important to intimately understand the relationship God wants you to have with your spouse.

Question Nineteen

What is God's purpose for marriage?

Now we all know the Sunday school answer to this question. God tells us in Genesis 1:28 to be fruitful and multiply and fill the earth. But as we parents can attest that, there is more to married life than making and raising babies. As enjoyable an activity as it is, this plays a small role in the relationship as a whole. God's purpose for marriage is for companionship. God created men to excel in certain aspects of life euphemistically called the *heavy lifting,* while women have been blessed with the natural gifting of nurturing and care giving. Not only has God delicately hand crafted the world in which we live; He placed particular care in ensuring that his creatures are cared for. Even more so, as God placed humankind in charge of all His creation, He wanted to make sure that we were well cared for as well. In doing so, He created a partnership between man and woman that would allow them to work hand in hand to fulfil God's plan.

Question Twenty

What is God's role in your current life/relationship?

In our opinion, all of the preceding nineteen questions will have little bearing on the success of your marriage unless you get this one *right*. The role that God has in your personal life and in your relationship will dictate the success or failure of your relationship. If you are to be successful under the covenant of marriage ordained by God, it stands to reason that a certain degree of effort be invested towards an established relationship with Him.

Let's begin with your personal relationship with the Author and Finisher of your faith (Hebrews 12:2). First things first, do you have one? The best way to measure God's role in your life is to measure how much time you spend with Him. Having a full-time job, a few kids, taking an active role in your church along with a long list of personal interests, can make it difficult to take time solely devoted to God. But we also know how much time we are able to find to listen to music, talk on the phone, watch TV or check our Facebook.

After enduring the potentially long and often painful process of unplugging yourself from these things, you will find as we did, that you have the time to strengthen the relationship with the Lord of your life. Do we really need to know what that person was dying of on your favourite medical drama? Do we really need to spend more time on the computer at home after spending most of the day on the computer at work?

You will find that as you give these once wasted moments to the Lord, He will use them to draw you closer to Him. The payoff will be the more time that you spend with God, the stronger your relationship will grow with your partner. It has become discernable to each of us now in our relationship when we have been spending time building up God's kingdom and when we have been building our own. Remember that the Scriptures tell us that we serve a jealous God who desperately wants us to serve Him. Spending time with God is like sitting out in the sun on a warm spring day. The more time you spend in the sun, the more you will display the effects of its rays. Such is the case with spending time with God. The more time you spend in His Word, praying, praising and worshipping, the more radiant a reflection you will be of His light.

As a couple, if you truly desire to be successful in your marriage you must present your relationship before God. Firstly, be certain your relationship is blessed with His anointing. As king David often said, there is nothing that we can do to win God's favour if we are not obedient to His will. He also wrote that he had never seen the righteous forsaken (Psalm 37:25). As we walk uprightly before God and are obedient to His Word, he will not turn us away.

God is not concerned with how attracted you

are to your partner. His priority is not whether you can carry on a stimulating conversation, volunteer together at a soup kitchen or enjoy taking long walks together along the beach. God doesn't even care if you are both living a life dedicated to serving Him, if it is not in His will for you both to be together, your relationship simply will not work. This truth is not only reflected in the alarming divorce rate in North America, it is reflected in the tragic divorce rate among Christ following Christians.

If you have aligned yourselves with the will of God, forming a threefold cord that cannot be easily broken (Ecclesiastes 4:12 NKJV), and are prepared to fight for each other rather than against each other, then you have laid the foundation of a godly and successful marriage.

Chapter *Eight*

What Marriage Is

Also, if two lie down together, they will keep warm.
But how can one keep warm alone? Though one
may be overpowered, two can defend themselves.
A cord of three strands is not quickly broken.
Ecclesiastes 4:11-12

We often liken the married couple to laborers dressed in hard hats complete with steel-toed boots, a tool belt and a metal lunch pail. Maintaining a strong and godly marriage requires us to work hard *everyday*. Marriage is a relationship that requires couples to be present and willing to give their very best effort. Marriage is also a relationship of seasons. There are seasons of abundant sunshine and joy, but there are also times of rain storms and despair. As God enables in those troubling seasons, stick with it. As the Bible tells us weeping may endure for a night, but joy comes in the morning (Psalm 30:5 NKJV). The beauty of marriage is that the sun will shine through after you weather the storm. As long as you walk hand in hand through the storm together with your eyes fixed on God.

Marriage is Weathering the Storm

When the storm is raging you may feel as though you need a life raft to take you to safety and perhaps away from your marriage. In fact we do need a life raft, but not only when the storm is raging, we need one all the time. Our life raft is the Holy Spirit. He is our Counselor. He is that little voice inside, or the still small voice that says "No, not here" or "Yes, go there." The Holy Spirit when invited into your marriage will always guard it, protect it, and preserve it. This is why He is our life raft in times of trouble. When people are lost at sea, the rescuers that come in the mist of the storm are called Guardians. This is what the Holy Spirit wants to do for you.

Unfortunately, often times married people take refuge in places outside their marriage. This may come in many forms. It may be putting in those extra hours at work to secure that promotion, hanging out watching the game with friends, or spending time with that co-worker who gives you that *extra* attention. Understand that these things are mere distractions. What we need to do in the storm is stand. "Therefore my dear brothers, stand firm, let nothing move you. Always give yourselves fully to the work of the Lord, because you know that your labor in the Lord is not in vain" (1Corinthians 15:58).

Marriage is the Lord's work. The marriage is the foundation of the family, the family the foundation of society. This is what God intended when He established marriage. The erosion of marriage has lead to so many of the ills we see reflected around us. God intends for us to stand and labor through whatever difficulties arise in marriage. He also promises to never leave us as we labor. When you have done all you are able to do, stand – God will do the rest. "Therefore put on the full armor of God, so that when the day of evil comes, you may be able to stand your ground, and after you have done everything to stand" (Ephesians 6:13).

Marriage is a Selfless Act

To marry someone is a selfless act. I once heard a man say on a talk show that he is happily married because he learned to die to himself. The talk show host said she had never heard it said that way. She and her guests who were divorced or never been married said it should not have to be this way. The man who made the statement was also divorced and attributed his divorce in part to his selfishness. Now remarried, he and his wife have taken a selfless, die-to-self approach to their Christ-centered marriage. You could see their joy. Yet this selfless approach to marriage gets a knee jerk reaction that says, "No! I can still be an individual, I can still have my own separate stuff, I should not have to reform or conform to this other person." But the one who created marriage, established it in this way, the man and woman are to rule over the created order of things on the earth "for this reason a man will leave his father and mother and be united to his wife, and they will become one flesh" (Genesis 2:24).

To marry someone is indeed a selfless act. To marry someone is to say I will put you first; your needs go before mine. First Corinthians 7:4 tells us that the wife's body does not belong to her alone but also to her husband. In the same way, the husband's body does not belong to him alone but also to his wife. That is contrary to our nature as fallen humans, particularly in this "me first" postmodern world we live in today. We believe that if we don't secure our own needs then they won't be looked after. This is true in most of our relationships unfortunately. However, there is no place for this mindset in marriage. When both spouses take the "you first" approach, then marriage is a joy. When your spouse is able to trust that you put her first, she will absolutely give you her everything. But our thinking is backwards, like the guests on the talk show, mentioned earlier, we think we have to do for ourselves first in marriage to get our needs met. Instead, the very thing that you want and need you must be willing to give away first. Then it comes right back to you double portion. Jesus taught that we should give and it will be given to you, a good measure, pressed down shaken together and running over (Luke 6:38). That sounds like more than a double portion! Imagine all the love, acceptance, forgiveness, trust and freedom you need in such measure that when it is pressed down and shaken together it will continue to overflow into your lap! This is what happens when you give all of *you* to your spouse, but in order to do this you will have to die to self.

Marriage is Engaging in Battle

Your marriage truly begins after you have made the commitment to remain together whatever comes. Before that moment when you spiritually and emotionally make that commitment, we believe your marriage still only exists on a trial basis. The traditional vows have included staying together for richer or for poorer, in sickness and in health, in other words, for better or worse. However, it is easy to allow ourselves to become emotionally discontent. A feeling that we are not getting what we want from our marriage and that our needs are not being met can lead to an emotional separation between husband and wife. If allowed to linger in your home for even one day, emotional separation can lead to the eventual demise of your marriage. Remember, the enemy hates that which God holds dear. God loves marriage and He created it to spare us from loneliness. God hates divorce, whether it is legal or emotional. Satan hates marriage. He loves divorce.

We need to understand that to maintain our relationship and provide stability and security for ourselves and our children, we have enlisted in spiritual warfare. The Bible tells us that our struggle is not against flesh and blood but against the rulers, against the authorities, against the powers of this dark world and against the spiritual forces of evil in the heavenly realms (Ephesians 6:12). So you see, not only is your marriage a spiritual covenant, it also involves waging spiritual warfare. There are dark forces at work against you and your spouse that you cannot see, but they are very much at work.

One way to combat the problem of emotional separation is to take preventative measures. We all know what triggers our spouse to become angry or defensive or whatever the case may be. If you are newly married you will eventually learn these through time and close observation. With this in mind, ask yourself in every situation, "Is what I am about to say helpful or hurtful to my spouse?" A good question to ask yourself in the heat of the moment is, "Will my actions and words bring life or death to my relationship with my spouse?" These are tough questions to examine when you really just want to "blow off some steam." But if your words or actions will bring your spouse hurt and death (in a spiritual sense), then prevent the course of emotional separation upon which you are about to embark. "Blowing off steam" is never worth this painful journey. It is difficult to do, but anyone who has been divorced or close to it will tell you that it is far easier to prevent a problem than to work through one once a problem becomes chronic. Usually by the time emotional distance becomes a way of life for couples, there is little strength left to fight and the enemy has you pinned.

Marriage is Navigating Troubled Waters

However, when sin in us takes over and we hurt our spouse it is important to repent and seek forgiveness quickly. It is equally important to respond with grace and forgiveness when we have been wronged.

Now there is nothing wrong with being proactive once you find yourself in troubled waters, but it is better to avoid the trouble altogether. None of us will be a perfect spouse but our goal should be to be like Jesus who was perfect in all his ways (Matthew 5:48). When you find yourself in troubled waters with your spouse, seek forgiveness and never tire of doing right as 2 Thessalonians 3:13 tells us.

Remember scripture tells us, not to let the sun go down while we are still angry (Ephesians 4:26). Do not fall into silence and distance when you have been wronged. This is so painful, especially for children who come from families where this is the everyday dynamic between their parents. They live in homes where there is no display of love. We all were created to need love. We were created to be in relationship. For children to witness an emotional void between their parents does just that, it leaves a void. In addition, participating in emotional distance leaves a void in you. It is lonely, tiring and gets you nowhere; it takes you prisoner. When you have done wrong seek forgiveness and do right. When you have been wronged extend grace and forgiveness.

Avoid emotional distance from your spouse at all costs. It is that emotional connection that brought you together in the first place. Emotional distance opens the door to the enemy and gives him a foothold in your marriage. A foothold is like an opening. The devil seeks this out in us individually and as a couple. Once he has found this opening, he can enter in and wreak havoc. Remember, the devil hates marriage, he hates your love, and he hates your union. But the Bible says God hates divorce (Malachi 2:16). He loves your marriage, He loves your love, and He loves your union. He has a plan to prosper you now and in the future (Jeremiah 29:11), but He must be the center of your relationship. We must build a fence around our family on the foundation of God's Word, the creator of marriage.

Apart from God, marriage cannot be experienced as He fully intends. It matters little how things look on the outside to others. God created us to be in relationship with Him and our "Spiritmate". We cannot replicate authentic marriage without the Architect (God) or the blueprint (His Word). We would not dream of building a house without a design or blueprints, but we erroneously believe that marriage can stand without being under Christ's control and direction. God is calling us back to His heart for what marriage is.

Chapter *Nine*

What Marriage Is *Not*

Marriage should be honored by all...
Hebrews 13:4

Now that we have discussed what marriage *is*, we will now discuss what marriage is *not*. In this chapter, we seek to debunk what we believe to be general myths about what marriage *is*. Specifically, we will focus on six of the most common factors that have *mis*led couples down the aisle.

Marriage is not a way to escape from home

Firstly, marriage is not a means to escape from your parental home. This may be hard for some to hear because after all only you know the struggles you face at home. But while this may be true, getting married is not the way to solve the problems you may be experiencing. It is certainly difficult for some to be an adult living in your parents' home. This can be especially challenging if your parents still think of you and treat you like a child. However, running from your parents' home into a marriage without the proper preparation, counsel and prayer is one of the worst things a young person can do. This often is a set up for disaster. It *is* possible to leave home with unresolved issues with your parents and pursue your marriage. Mind you, it is not the best way to start your new life. However with proper preparation, counsel and earnest prayer, it is possible to move forward in getting married.

So what are we saying here? Under no circumstances should you marry someone to escape a difficult home life. In our chapter on Motives, we explored individuals' intentions for getting married. Being in love is a gift from our heavenly Father, but pursuing marriage with the wrong motives is a guarantee for many miserable days and quite possibly a miserable life. Marrying someone with the right motives, with proper preparation, counsel and prayer, even in the midst of a difficult home life, you can still lead to a joy-filled married life. For example, Jacob has a parent who is an abusive alcoholic. But he has been actively working to overcome the effects of growing up in such a family. With prayer, pre-marital counseling and personal devotion to God's Word; he can still look forward to a healthy marriage.

Marriage is not a way to escape from a bad situation

Similar to marriage not being an escape from your parental home, it is also not to be used as an escape from a bad situation. For example, if an unwed couple finds themselves facing an unplanned pregnancy, they are often given the advice to get married. Please understand, we do not encourage that more children be raised in this fatherless generation. It is our belief that the marriage is the foundation of the family and the family is the foundation of society. Marriage is an essential part of our social fabric. However, couples should not get married for the wrong reasons. God's Word tells us that marriage is to be honored.

Each couple who finds themselves in a particularly difficult situation will have to navigate their way through in order to arrive at the decision that is the right one. It is important to reiterate that marriage does not fix what you or others may deem to be a mistake or an unfortunate situation. In fact, there is more pressure on these marriages to make them work if the foundation has been poorly laid. Again, for your situation, seek out a person with wisdom who can help you navigate through it. If marriage is what you seek, you have to be properly prepared particularly in light of your situation. Remember your marriage must be rooted in love, bound by commitment and sanctioned by God.

Marriage is not a way to fix your financial woes

Marriage is also *not* a means by which to fix financial woes. It has been said that if you marry for money you earn every penny of it. The Bible tells us that, the love of money is the root of all evil, and that some people, eager for money, have wandered from the faith and pierced themselves with many griefs (1Timothy 6:10). This tells us clearly that when you put yourself in a position to acquire money through dishonorable means, you will find yourself "pierced with many griefs". If two people come together as a way to satisfy monetary gain this indicates that the object of affection is money not the person you intend to marry. If the object of affection is money, this is evil. If a marriage is rooted in and founded on evil it will very likely turn into a grievous situation for both parties. Marriage cannot be established apart from how the Architect intends, otherwise it will not stand.

Marriage is not a way to have a convenient roommate

In the book of Genesis, God surveys all of creation, including man and says, "It is not good for man to be alone. I will make a helper suitable for him" (Genesis 2:18). God in his graciousness knows our needs and makes provision for us. He knew that the man would be lonely not having one of his own kind, not only to share the work of caring for creation, but also to share his life and his heart. Although the man was in perfect communion with God and God in perfect communion with the man, God created woman – *for* man to ease his loneliness.

This being said, there is no disputing that one of the wonderful benefits of marriage is that it protects us from loneliness. Having someone to share your life and heart with is something that God honors so much so that He included it as part of the blueprint for building marriage. God specifically mentions this provision for loneliness in His Word. In this fallen world, unfortunately, we sometimes use something that God has ordained to meet our selfish desires. Taking a spouse as a convenient roommate, someone to do the laundry and pick up the dry cleaning or help to parent children from a previous relationship is not what God intended when He created marriage.

Earlier we discussed how marrying someone is an act of selflessness. To be selfless is to regard your spouse before yourself. It is to say, "How can I serve you?", rather than "How can I be served?" The isolation a person can feel when living with a selfish spouse can create a greater sense of loneliness than being single and alone. So marriage ought not to be a way to "lock in" a roommate, instead it should be two individuals coming together as teammates.

Marriage is not a way to lawfully consummate your relationship

Particularly in Christian circles many couples get married too quickly in order to lawfully consummate their relationship. Seeking to surrender the physical aspect of the relationship to God and remaining pure until marriage is honorable. There would be a much smoother transition into the sexual relationship of a couple's marriage if they chose to surrender to Christ's control completely in this area. The spiritual baggage that the couple that chooses not to wait brings to their marriage can lead to their undoing. There is often guilt, remorse and unnatural soul ties that have been formed as a result of premarital sexual relations.

We will later discuss in more detail the mess couples coming together for sexually gratification can find themselves in. For the purpose of the discussion about what marriage is not; it should absolutely *not* be a way simply to consummate the relationship. Sexual intimacy can be the overshadowing thought or feeling between two people who are in love. Sexual thoughts can really dominate a couple's courtship to the exclusion of many other important aspects of what marriage entails. What is likely to happen with couples who almost exclusively base their marriage on the act of consummation is that they quickly find that a relatively small fraction of their marriage is actually spent in the marital bed. Most of our time as couples is spent negotiating one situation after another, whether it is chores around the house, paying bills, running errands, or working. Sexual intimacy draws couples close so that they can negotiate life outside the bedroom. Yet, it cannot be the basis upon which the couple comes together. If the couple does not have a firm foundation upon which the relationship is built, the desire for sexual intimacy will begin to fade. If there is no preparation to negotiate the other key elements of a life together, sex will become the last thing on your spouse's mind.

Time on its own prepares you for nothing. There are couples whose courtship lasted a few short months and go on to be committed to one another for a lifetime. Conversely, there are couples whose courtship last for a couple of years but find themselves unable to navigate through the marital relationship. Truthfully, it is the work that goes into getting ready for the "big life" after the "big day", that will determine if a couple succeeds or fails particularly in the first two years. This is a critical time and many marriages dissolve after less than the two year mark due to lack of planning, preparation and commitment.

Marriage is not an item on life's "to do" list

You may know someone who thinks she should get married because she is at *that* age. Suddenly the pressure is on to find Mr. Right. There really isn't a certain age by which anyone should get married. There isn't an invisible finish line that people of that *certain age* need to cross with a spouse in tow. Thinking this way is a bad idea. God will provide you with the spouse He has chosen for you. Be patient. Waiting on the Lord can be difficult but on this issue (and on all issues truthfully), but it is always worth it in the end. The most important decision you will make in your life is the decision to follow Jesus Christ and make him the Lord of your life. The second most important decision you will make is who you choose to marry – so choose well.

Chapter *Ten*

The Five Factors
that Impact Marriage

*But those who marry will face many troubles
in this life, and I want to spare you this.*
1 Corinthians 7:28

There are five factors that will impact your marriage. These five factors affect couples at different stages of their marriage, whether they are a newly married couple or have been married for decades. The five factors deal with sex, money, roles, parenting and in-laws. Take roles for example, many couples have a lot of assumptions about who will do what. But most couples have had little conversation about who will be responsible for what tasks and how labor in the family will be divided.

As is true with roles, sex is a key component to the marital puzzle. Couples need to be honest with one another in discussing their expectations in this area. In today's society, sex can carry with it a lot of shame, but the marriage bed is one to be celebrated

(Genesis 2:25). Honesty, honor, respect and transparency promote a healthy sex life between a husband and wife.

Money is another key issue that needs to be discussed often, using open, productive dialogue. There is a lot of dishonesty and secrecy with regard to money in our society. People will often fabricate how much they make, their net worth, or their debt load to paint themselves in a better light. Unfortunately, this deception is taken into too many marriages. This is no way to begin a life with one another. Financial issues, including budgeting, debts, spending habits, hobbies, history and feelings around money *must* all be discussed prior to your marriage. These discussions also need to take place on an ongoing basis as part of a healthy marriage.

Parenting obviously becomes an issue once a couple has children, but it still needs to be a key area of deep exploration during the pre-marital period. Assumptions about parenting should never be made. For example, there shouldn't be the assumption that your partner wants children because you do. Nor should you assume that you and your partner want the same number of children or have similar philosophies about discipline. In our courtship, we discussed having two children and planned to wait for five years before starting a family to give us time to establish ourselves as a couple. After three years Sara really wanted to have a baby, this is where flexibility comes in. With God's blessing we conceived and had our first born, Caleb. But we had to negotiate whether Sara would go back to work or stay home when our daughter Eden was born. We both had made assumptions around our parenting and we were both very wrong. Again this is where flexibility comes in. We had to come up with a balance between working and staying home and we often had to revisit how to strike that balance. This issue should be negotiated so you are both on the same page. It can't be overstated; nothing around children and child rearing should be assumed.

Our experience with this has taught us how important it is to talk things out thoroughly, not to make assumptions, but to also be flexible because change happens. Most importantly we needed to surrender both our wills to the Lord Jesus and allow Him to show us what is best for our family. As we did this, He began to show us His plan for our family. We knew we had to surrender completely in this area. As in all areas, with complete submission we are able to find peace as well as the answers we are looking for.

Finally, negotiating the relationships with relatives, extended family or 'in-laws' can be unbearable for some couples. Establishing healthy boundaries will help to protect the couple and allow them to filter these outside influences. Boundaries in a family are like fences, they keep the good things in and the bad things out.

Let's look more closely at the first of the Five Factors that will impact your marriage.

Chapter *Eleven*

Sex

How can a young man keep his way pure?
By living according to your word.
Psalm 119:9

Joyfully for some young couples, sex will be a new experience for them. Many couples wait for that special someone the Lord has chosen for them. The importance of purity before marriage cannot be overstated. This is preached from the pulpit in evangelical churches and drilled into young people during their pre-marital counseling. The issue of purity is also discussed in youth groups and on retreats. Yet in our experience in working with young people, often they are *not* waiting until they get married before their relationship becomes sexual.

Many couples who have had premarital sex have found that their experiences have had a detrimental effect on the intimacy of their marriage. Yet young people often ask, "Why wait? Everyone is doing it." We have even heard young people say, "Many people are getting married to the wrong person just so they can do it *lawfully*." We have already touched on this issue in our discussion about what marriage is not. However, to answer the question, it is alarming the far-reaching effects that this sin can have on our lives. Paul said it best when he wrote, "Flee from sexual immorality. All other sins a man commits are outside his body, but he who sins sexually sins against his own body" (1Corinthians 6:18).

God has said in His Word that the marriage bed is to be kept pure (Hebrews 13:4). Sex is intended by God as a part of marriage for us to procreate, and to experience pleasure and intimacy. This is most pleasing to God. When we cheat and begin a sexual relationship with someone who is not our spouse, not only do we displease God, but we leave ourselves open to the consequences of our sin. These include unwanted pregnancies, sexually transmitted infections, and deep-rooted shame. Do you see the polar opposite results that we experience when we do things our way instead of God's way? Instead of producing children out of love we find ourselves with children we do not want. Instead of pleasure we get disease and instead of closeness, there is separation. This is the scheme of the devil, who seeks to rob you of all the good things that come out of enjoying sex with your spouse. Jesus said, "The thief comes only to steal, kill and destroy; I have come that they (meaning those who believe in Him) may have life, and have it to the full" (John 10:10). We receive His life when we are obedient to His ways.

There are a countless number of ways that sex before marriage can lead to the demise of intimacy after you are married. The guilt and shame that are attached to premarital sex is overwhelming and can literally drive a wedge between two people who once loved each other with great passion. So please wait. God will be pleased and you won't be sorry. His Word is clear; flee from sexual immorality.

Throwing off that which hinders

Has God ever told you to get rid of something from your past? By this we mean things in your past that bear a symbol of disobedience to God. We believe that God speaks in a clear, persistent, voice about this. The Word tells us to "throw off everything that hinders and the sin that so easily entangles, and let us run with perseverance the race marked out for us" (Hebrews 12:1).

A symbol of disobedience may be someone you had a relationship with other than your spouse prior to your marriage. Whether this encounter leads to sexual sin, or it was simply a crush, the memories of this encounter need to be surrendered to God. There are people, places and things that leave an imprint on us. There comes a time, that in order to move deeper and closer in our relationship with God and with our partner we must as Scripture tells us, throw off everything that hinders. This may include individuals with whom you have had a relationship with in the past. These relationships may be preventing you from walking in the fullness of what God has called you to in your relationship now. We often have a good idea of what is detrimental to our relationships. Therefore, it is our responsibility to begin to remove the obstacles that hinder the sexual health of marriage.

We encourage you to keep reading even if what we are discussing now does not directly relate to you or your partner. We have started this chapter on sex with this disclaimer to throw off everything that hinders, because as we have talked to couples and singles over the years, we have found that in the area of sexuality, many people are bound. This entanglement often results from premarital sexual encounters that have created a stronghold. While the Word of God has remained unchanged on the matter, we as a church have been slow to receive the protection the Lord provides us when He designated sex for marriage only. In other words, disobedience in the area of sexuality in the church is rampant and it is destroying marriages before they have a chance to even begin.

We create ties with others in our lives that have a healing or destructive power. When the Holy Spirit speaks to you about removing something that hinders and easily entangles we must be obedient. This may be some sin, but can also be a romantic relationship that has long been over, but has left an indelible mark on us. Submit this to the Lord Jesus and He will remove or break this bond. This is how we move into intimacy, not only with our partner, but also with our God. By this act of submission, we are able to move closer together in intimacy and we are able to weather the storms that come in the various seasons of marriage.

Seasons change

There have been seasons in our marriage that have been painful. There have been times we were certain we would not be able bear up under the strain. But in times like these Jesus reminds us that "my grace is sufficient for you and my power is made perfect in weakness" (2 Corinthians 12:9). In times like these you may even question what brought you together as a couple in the first place.

It is in these times that your partner is feeling the most vulnerable; perhaps even unloved, unlovable, angry or depressed. What we often do in these valley times is withdraw from our spouse emotionally and especially physically. Say a couple has an argument about work, or money or their in-laws, whatever it is, after the heated exchange both parties go to their separate corners. This happens because feelings are hurt. We go our separate ways in part to tend to the wounds our partner may have inflicted.

Now this is natural, it is human. What is unnatural is to stay in those "corners" for hours, days or even weeks. What this leads to is bitterness, resentment and most of all, unforgiveness begins to ferment. When given too much time and attention, these negative feelings can fester and take on a life of their own. It can even become a part of a couple's new identity. What was once a warm loving partnership can quickly sour, if partners separate from one another and detach emotionally and sexually.

Sexual relations suffer at times like these for many couples. Especially for women whose readiness for a sexual encounter with her husband has much to do with the emotional connectedness she feels with him. This is why the Scriptures encourage us to not let the sun go down while we are still angry. It further admonishes us to not give the devil a foothold in our relationship (Ephesians 4:26-27). We have discussed this before, about giving the devil a foothold and how dangerous this is. Have we gone to bed angry in our years of marriage? Sure. Does this practice cause a problem to fester and further divide us? Absolutely! So it is always best to lay pride aside and reconcile before a new day begins. We had to learn this the hard way.

When we withdraw from our spouse after an argument, or for an extended period of time, the devil thoroughly enjoys this. We provide him with a portal or an opening to come in a wreak havoc in our marriage. After a brief cooling off period, it is important to resume connection and intimacy as soon as possible. This includes talking things through, calmly listening to what your partner has to say, seeking and giving forgiveness and then physical intimacy can resume. This is how God intends for us to be deeply connected to our spouse.

God designed sex to reflect the depth of love He has for us. He desires true intimacy and unity with us and he allows us to express this spiritual connection with one another in marriage. Sexual intimacy helps the couple to fortify their commitment to growing deeper spiritually with one another. You see, in order to achieve true intimacy we cannot be angry, unforgiving or judgmental of our spouse. We have to put the negative emotions aside to make room for positive ones. As we do this continually, our marriage is strengthened and congealed.

Expectation and Communication

Before couples are married, it is important to have an honest and balanced conversation about sexual expectations. What has been harmful to young people and couples is the lopsided discussion about sex that takes place in some of our churches. The extent of the discussion in many Christian circles is to "wait until you are married." Of course we support this position, because this is our Heavenly Father's position. However, in our experience, more needs to be said on the subject. In our own marriage and in our discussions with other couples, one of the first areas of concern that arises in the marriage is the issue of sex.

While sex is not something the engaged couple should be doing, it is definitely something that they should be talking about — a lot. This is where many people will start to go quiet. We believe we do not talk about sex freely in evangelical circles out of fear. There is the fear that if we talk about sex a lot with unwed young people and young couples, this will encourage them to explore their sexuality. Well let's put this out there. Many, many, many young couples are having sex even if it is one time before they get married. Quite frankly *our* fear is *our* reality.

The reason we need to talk about expectations and how to communicate them, is because this will help you once you are married. Many couples get married to have sex, only to find out that they are cleaning the house, paying bills, working and doing the grocery shopping far more than they are having sex. Sex is a reflection of the intimacy that a couple *already* shares in non-sexual areas of the relationship. It cannot, nor can ever be the foundation of a couple's relationship. It cannot be the reason two people come together, because it is only a matter of time before disappointment and resentment set in. So with that said, let's talk about sex.

Sexual Adjustment in Marriage

We live in a sex-crazed generation. No time than ever before has there been more explicit sexual content in our culture. We are bombarded by television, advertisements and the Internet. Yet the church remains silent on the subject. You may not be able to recall hearing one sermon preached on the Song of Solomon. Yet sex was created by God as a beautiful expression of love. One of our hopes in writing to you is that there will be an increase in healthy dialogue among singles, couples, pastors and counselors to demystify the subject of sex.

Whether or not couples have remained pure until their wedding night, there is certainly an adjustment to the new sexual relationship as husband and wife. Moving forward, we will discuss sexual adjustment as a new sexual experience.

We are created by God as sexual beings. Sex was created by God for the purpose of bringing about a deep spiritual connection between a husband and his wife. Sex draws a couple closer into the state of being one flesh, more so than any other activity in their marital life. We believe this is God's heart and his desire for marriage.

A couple can provide wonderful pleasure to one another in a variety of different ways. In the sex life of a married couple, we can do so without modesty. Modesty is something women especially are encouraged to practice because it guards her Christian brother from lust. Just as Christian men are cautioned not to take that *second glance* leading their minds down a dangerous path towards lust and adultery. These instructions however, are not meant to be brought into the sexual relationship of married couples.

Until a couple becomes husband and wife modesty in dress and behavior is important because it encourages sexual purity. It can be difficult to transition from the modesty that is expected before marriage into the intimacy that is required to build a strong sexual relationship in marriage. We believe there are five principles that couples can follow in this area. First explore one another, also take time with one another, romance one another, connect with one another and touch one another.

First *explore*. On many a wedding night there is the apprehension about having sex for the first time. Especially if there has not been a lot of discussion about sex beyond, "I can't wait until we can have sex!" If the couple has waited this long to consummate the relationship on the wedding night, there really needs to be no rush. Many people get the Hollywood or the

Harlequin image of couples making mad passionate love; each aching to be ravished. This image should really be discarded once and for all. Sex in marriage should be seen as more of an act of worship to our Creator. Instead of picturing Matthew Macconaughey or Jessica Alba in their latest romantic comedy, picture that you and your spouse are in intimate worship. So take the time to explore your spouse's body, her face and hands and feet — all of her. Take her in; she is yours and you are hers.

The next point to consider is, *take time*. There is no rush. Rushing into intercourse to get to the finish would be like rushing through your devotions. Remember this is a form of worship. The way men and women experience a sexual encounter in very different. Men are aroused more quickly while women need more time to get prepared for intimacy. For men the act of intercourse dominates his thoughts while women are more focused on the entire experience. For her this includes love play (loving interactions prior to love making) and foreplay (physical exploration during the sexual encounter) that lead up to sexual intercourse. This is why taking it slow allows for both partners to achieve sexual satisfaction. It is a wonderful way to meet the needs of both the woman as well as the man leading up to and including intercourse. Taking your time allows for far more fulfilling love making. When love making takes place in a romantic setting the experience is more gratifying. So be sure to take the time to set the right tone.

Romance is key. Romance means to woo or make

love. When you romance your spouse you are beckoning him to you so that you can lavish love on him. This lies at the heart of intimacy. When your spouse knows that she is being drawn to you to be *given* love she will come to you every time. Romance includes buying flowers or cooking a candlelight dinner, this is how married couples lavish love on one another.

Couples also need to *connect.* We certainly wish we knew this earlier in our marriage. Connecting is vital. Eye-gazing is an invaluable connecting tool. It has been said that the eyes are the windows to the soul. Gaze into your spouse's eyes for several minutes without looking away as part of foreplay. We believe when you do this, it allows you to *see* your spouse. Not as a sexual object who is now here to meet your sexual needs at last, but as a person, as another spiritual being just like you. You may develop other ways to connect with your spouse that work well for you. The important thing is to take time to connect.

Finally couples are to *touch.* There is an instant connection when two people touch. My wife has this habit of touching people as they come into and leave her presence. She does this all day long with our children. They come up to her and ask her something and she touches them, they go off to play and she touches them. A touch says, "I acknowledge you, you have my undivided attention and moreover, I want to impart some love to you." With a simple touch we are connected to another person. For couples a touch displaces separateness and creates oneness.

We can all attest to the power of an affirming touch. Newborn babies who have not been touched will eventually die even if they are fed. Likewise, this is why it is so important in establishing intimacy with your spouse, both sexually and non-sexually using touch.

Having said all this, we understand that there is a biological component to sexual adjustment in marriage. Some couples marry with very little knowledge about male and female anatomy and physiology. Couples in this position should do a lot of reading about how sexual relations physically take place and ask lots of questions of their pre-marital counselor. What we have discussed here are some emotional components that go hand in hand with, and facilitate the physical side of sex.

Couples reading this who have already experienced sex together prior to your marriage should still take note of the five principles we have discussed and implement them into your new sexual relationship. Your marriage is a new covenant that God wants to bless. He can put all past mistakes as far as the east is from the west if you and your partner go to Him sincere and repentant. Past sin does not have to hinder your future. God wants you to see your sex life together as an act of worship.

Chapter *Twelve*

Finances

I know what it is to be in need, and I know what it is to have plenty. I have learned the secret of being content in any and every situation, whether well fed or hungry, whether living in plenty or in want.
Philippians 4:12

Marriage is a partnership. In the area of finances the need for true partnership is of the utmost importance. When two lives become one, not only do they share their lives they share their possessions. Many couples struggle in the area of finances. Many of us were not given adequate tools to handle money. We simply do not know how money works. Budgeting, investing, saving it, can all be daunting.

What couples need before they take the step into marriage is a financial plan. This plan should include a family or household budget. This budget directs how the income that comes into that home will be spent. The Bible admonishes that we cannot love both God and money (Matthew 6:24). However, a plan about money and extensive discussions about money during engagement should not be confused with an obsession with money. Many couples overlook seeking helpful guidance about money at crucial times such as during engagement, because the focus is on the relationship and growing deeper in love. Also for many people discussions about money is still taboo. So to be clear, discussions about your financial future are important and God-honoring. It shows that the couple is willing to be transparent on all levels and this is essential in building the foundation for a strong marriage. Remember, God calls us to be good financial stewards.

Financial Essentials

There are two fundamentals a couple needs to be aware of with regard to finances in your new marriage. First there must be accountability. Mutual financial accountability can be a difficult concept for some couples to take hold of; especially if they have been living by themselves for a few years and have become financially self-reliant. What couples ought to realize is that once we get married, we no longer can be concerned with individual wealth, but must now understand that we are a team that supports each other financially. This leads to the next fundamental which is dependence on one another; there is no "I" in team. As part of a couple you no longer spend money exclusively on the things that *I* want. There needs to be consensus on what purchases are made, especially large ones. As a result there is some reduced financial independence.

For richer or for poorer

In Philippians 4:12 Paul pens, "I know what it is to be in need, and I know what it is to have plenty. I have learned the secret of being content in any and every situation, whether well fed or hungry, whether living in plenty or in want." Couples take hold of this truth. Often times, when couples experience financial difficulty for the first time, they tend to take out their frustrations on each other. We often lose sight of the vow we took to love each other for richer or for poorer. Financial security symbolizes emotional security for many people. In other words, many people feel that when they have a certain amount of money, they will experience emotional well-being. It is like the wife who says, "When we pay off this credit card I can finally stop worrying about money and just relax", or the husband who says, "When I finally get this next raise we can breathe easier." Then to their surprise, the card gets paid off and the raise comes yet there is still tension surrounding money.

Let us suggest that money is like a place. It is where people in relationships go to fight about deep-seated emotional issues. People think they will feel more secure the more money they have. This is a fallacy. That which created the insecurity in the first place will still be there if left unchecked. Money cannot solve emotional problems. Only God can.

Paul said to the Philippians that he learned the secret to being content regardless of his financial circumstances. This shows complete dependence on the Lord Jesus. Many engaged or newly married couples may not have a great deal of money to start married life with, but the secret to being content is to be dependent on our Lord to supply all our needs. As He supplied your need for companionship in your spouse, He will continue to supply all your needs as you trust Him and put Him first. All things we are able to do are through Christ. Overcoming emotional hurts and filling the void left by these hurts with relying on Jesus is the only way to be content whether we are in plenty or in want. When we live out this profound secret we find that we don't argue with our spouse about money when we are angry or hurt or disappointed about something else unrelated to money. We are able to indentify the true *dis*-ease and address it. If money is an issue that also needs to be addressed, it can be dealt with without all the emotions rooted in a deeper issue.

We have lived like this as a couple so we can attest that it is true. A couple can be in financial need and still be joyful and in love with each other. The Bible tells us that where our treasure is there our hearts will be also (Luke 12:34). In times of financial need we can only lean on God's promises to never leave us or forsake us (Deuteronomy 31:6). If a couple argues a lot about money, it is likely that the root issue is not being addressed and they are likely looking at their bank account more than they are looking to God. We will give you some practical tools to help you get on the right path.

Get a Financial Plan

We read in Proverbs 15:22 that plans fail for lack of counsel. While it is not helpful to worry or argue about money whether there is excess or lack, it is prudent to have a financial plan. The plan should be two fold. It should deal with how the couple's money will be tithed, spent, saved and invested. Also the plan must include accountability and mutual dependence; as previously discussed.

As we have stated, financial freedom is reduced once we enter into a marital covenant. While there are great financial benefits in marriage namely two incomes, or one spouse taking the role of primary caregiver while the other assumes the role of breadwinner, there is also a reduction in how freely each partner can spend the family's income. There needs to be accountability with how all the family's income is spent regardless of whether both spouses work outside the home full time. Many couples fall into an unhealthy pattern whereby only one spouse spends all the money and perhaps pays the bills while the other has no idea about the family's finances. The left hand does not know what the right hand is doing. Financially speaking this is a disastrous way to run a household. Each spouse must be willing and able to give an account of his or her spending habits. This shows mutual respect and establishes equality between the spouses. Also this encourages honesty. No marriage has ever failed because of this kind of sincere and loving honesty.

For couples adjusting to married life, this level of

accountability and mutual dependence can be difficult and downright frustrating at times. However,
this is a key area where surrender is required. When
each spouse is willing to die to their own egos the
marriage flourishes. Here again the two are becoming
one. This is at times, especially in the beginning of
marriage, a very painful process. However, the benefits far outweigh the sacrifices.

As part of the financial adjustment to married life,
couples should be specific when drawing up a budget.
You also need to have a philosophy about money.
Ours has become being good financial stewards. You
should spend your money wisely and do your best
to live below your means. History has shown us that
you cannot build your financial foundation on credit
and deception; eventually it will crumble all around
you. If you do not have the money in the bank, you
can't buy it. God is calling us back to good financial
stewardship where we put His interests first.

Chapter *Thirteen*

Roles

*It is better to trust the Lord
than to put confidence in man.
Psalm 118:8*

We have been taught, whether formally or informally, that gender and gender roles are socially constructed. By this we mean many people believe we as a society determine what gender is. That is to say what constitutes "maleness" or "femaleness". However, we know that God crafted our maleness and femaleness (Genesis 1:27). We also have been taught by our society that our roles in relationships, meaning our place or how we function, are assigned to us based on gender. There are cultures where women do the hunting and men do the childrearing. In other cultures the men are the breadwinners and women the homemakers. Regardless of the role we assume in our relationship with our partner, let us look at what the Scriptures tell us. It says that "it is better to trust the Lord than man" (Psalm 118:8). We tend to taint the fabric of our relationships due to our fallen selfish nature. We place expectations on one another, many times unwittingly, in order to promote our own selfish desires.

There is no place in a healthy marriage for unchecked selfish motivations. We must be present and conscious about how we engage one another in marriage. As you set out on this great marital adventure, discuss and explore your motivations for the roles you will assume in your new life together.

In marriage, it is far better to understand God's place for us in our relationship than the place assigned to us by others. You see God's motives are pure and His purposes are perfect. No earthly role we are ever assigned can give us this guarantee. With this as our backdrop there are some fundamental questions that couples should ask and answer about the roles they will assume in their marriage. For example, who should do what? Whose role is it biblically or historically to do what? Whose mother did what? Whose father did what? This issue of roles can require a United Nations mediator to help negotiate strategies for the new couple to maneuver! But this is the key point to consider — roles should not be assigned like a chore list on day one of your marriage. Marital roles should be negotiated.

Roles are Negotiated

What is for certain is that roles in marriage should be negotiated. Each couple is unique. Their marriage is unique and so are each spouse's personality, traits and family histories. We believe it is time to move away from the idea of *traditional* roles and move toward the idea of *negotiated* roles in marriage.

So what does this move entail? Well, each individual has a set of desires, hopes, aspirations, dreams and even fears. It is the role of a spouse to come alongside his wife and help to draw out what makes her unique and what purpose God has designed her to fulfill. A husband or a wife does this by first honoring the unique gifts, and inclinations of his or her spouse. People thrive in relationships where they are celebrated. As you continue to hold dear the traits and attributes of your spouse that caused you to fall in love with him in the first place, he feels honored as well as celebrated. It is unhelpful to pigeon-hole your spouse into roles he or she may not be suited for.

Early in our marriage, I could easily spend an entire Saturday afternoon watching weekend warrior, do-it-yourself type projects on television. I would then look over at my new husband and begin dreaming of him installing new cabinet doors and painting our apartment the perfect color. To my horror my husband simply had no interest in this kind of thing. Ask him a computer-related or "techy" question and his eyes would just light up. Then he would delve into his vast knowledge and answer your query in simple to understand language. Quite frankly this skill had no significance for me.

The way I felt about my husband's abilities became telling when our first apartment needed to be painted. I brought this set of assumptions about the work that needed to be done, *Our apartment needed painting and that is man's work.* Quite frankly

Robert would rather be raked over coals than spend a weekend painting. His solution was to hire a painter. Now, on a student budget this seemed insane to me but he would not budge. So with much reluctance on my part, we hired a painter.

I confess that this pattern of maintaining expectations of what was man's work and demanding that Robert do it plagued our marriage for years. Similarly, I was expected to do all the housework, meal preparation and overall household management. This is traditionally considered woman's work. We struggled with this because I really disliked housework and felt this should not be assigned to me purely on the basis of my gender. I often felt a sense of injustice. Yet, I was willing to inflict the same injustice on my spouse. This was a pattern we had to break.

It took a long time of going around in circles. We repeated the same demands and came up with the same resistance from one another until God began to show us that we had to stop it. It was time to apply our Vow to love, honor and cherish. What does God tell us about love in his Word? Love is patient. Love is kind…it is not self-seeking…it always protects (1 Corinthians 13:4-6).

When marriage begins there is a period of adjustment. Be patient with one another. This is love. While you are waiting to figure out how to live together day to day be kind. This is love. And when you begin to see the unique individual that God has created in your spouse resist the temptation to change her into someone more like you. Your spouse may not be good at everything but there are ways to negotiate which of you is better for certain tasks. This is true love. Finally, when your spouse becomes more vulnerable with you in sharing who he really is, you must protect his trust. This is love.

Over the course of your courtship we recommend playing the "Scenario Game". In the Scenario Game you come up with different scenarios to see how your partner would respond. So for example,

It's Saturday morning and we've had a busy week with work. The house is a mess, the shopping needs to be done and we have invited our in-laws over for dinner. How will we work together to have a great dinner party?

Now if you are courting and your partner is coming up empty in terms of suggestions, this is very telling about what your dynamic will be like given this inevitable situation. Whether male or female, if your spouse believes *you* should take care of everything while the other gets a spa treatment or watches the game, it is very likely that there will be tension by dinner time.

The point of the Scenario Game is to be honest about your answers and not just feed your partner what you think he may want to hear. Honesty is the best policy here. There is no point in getting all the answers right only to be weak on delivery once the "I dos" are in place. The Scenario Game can tell you so much of what your spouse actually expects from you, not only before you are married but after as well. Coming up with scenarios and seeking and giving honest answers is an amazing tool to gain insight into all of the Five Factors that will impact your marriage. The point of the game quite frankly is to uncover if you are marrying the right person and for right reasons. Exploration gives us clarity and lets us know if we are headed in the right direction.

Explore through Prayer

Prayer is the best form of exploration as we seek to know the heart of God for our relationships. When we go to God and express to Him our need for direction He will answer specifically in His time. The communication that you are seeking to build in your marital relationship should be a reflection of the communication that you have with Father God. Put another way, the communication that you have with Father God will be a reflection of the communication you will have in your marital relationship.

God in His infinite wisdom couples men and women together to complement one another. Where one is weak, the other is strong and vice versa. A husband who loves to cook may prepare most of the family meals. His wife may enjoy doing the gardening and the lawn care. How miserable would this couple be if they tried to get the other to do what "women are supposed to do" and what "men are supposed to do". Each couple will need to negotiate the terms of their marriage. God has established an order of things whereby the husband leads the family and the wife supports and nurtures. This was established for our benefit in marriage. However, a husband who leads can still scrub toilets and a wife who supports can still have a career.

Let us not substitute love and honor for tradition and duty. Let us not confuse the order that God has established in marriage with earthly tradition. Often young couples take on roles in their marriage that they feel expected by others to take on. In a sense, they perform a role as one would perform in a play. Performance is dangerous because by doing it we neglect to fully become who we are purposed by God to be. When we fail to be authentic in our relationships we create walls around us that do not allow love to flourish. Our heavenly Father who ordained and established marriage has the power and authority to help couples come together as one. But first we must seek Him prayerfully in everything.

The Roles to be Negotiated

We have struggled in this area of roles for many years because of the roles the church, as well as the world have set up for young couples. The truth is roles must be negotiated between two equals. The roles that specifically need to be negotiated in your relationship will present themselves as time goes on. However there are other roles, especially those which each of you really are passionate about, that should to be discussed thoroughly and honestly before your marriage.

If you are already married, take heart, it is never too late to make positive changes. Finally, as you take everything to the Lord in prayer you will discover that a spiritual intimacy develops in your home producing lasting love and lasting joy.

Chapter *Fourteen*

In-Laws

*Honor your father and mother which is the
first commandment with a promise, that it may
go well with you and that you may enjoy
long life on the earth.*
Ephesians 6:2

The families from which we came are to be celebrated, although combining *two* families can be
challenging. For many newly married couples this is
the greatest challenge they will face. One of the main
problems that couples have with their in-laws is rooted
in unhealthy attachments. There is a period of transition where our dependence on our parents needs to
change to interdependence with our spouse. The Bible
calls it leaving and cleaving (Genesis 2:24). This is
where we leave our parental home to cleave to our
spouse in order to establish our matrimonial home.
There are adult children about to get married or who
are newly married who still believe that their parents'
authority supersedes that of their spouse. Some parents
in fact feel this way as well. There are parents whose

adult children are about to get married or who are newly married who still act as though their authority takes pre-eminence. These are examples of unhealthy attachments. Unhealthy attachments will negatively affect the foundation of a couple's new marriage. This is why the Bible tells us how we should transition from one relationship to the other.

Once the transition into marriage takes place, we are told how the structure of our relationship with our spouse and relatives should look. The Bible says, "For the husband is the head of the wife as Christ is the head of the church, his body of which he is the Saviour" (Ephesians 5:23). It is unfortunate that this verse has been abused because it gives us the cornerstone principle of the way God intended us to "do" marriage. First He tells us the order of things. He clearly states who is to lead in the marital relationship. That is the husband. We struggled with this for years and years and some more years. It went against everything we learned from today's society. We are told that women are to be strong and independent, certainly not under any man.

However, this Scripture says nothing about a woman's inability to be strong. This verse highlights the order of the way things should be in a family. Every group must have a clear leader in order for their purpose to be carried out. The leader has a vision and he inspires those he is leading to catch his vision and help him carry it out. This is the role of the husband. The vision for his family comes from the Lord. The vision for all husbands whether they are in a relationship with Christ or not is to lead their families into the purpose of glorifying God on this earth.

The verse we have been discussing is not about putting a woman in "her place", or having a husband control his wife. Do not misunderstand. We must get this right in our own hearts before we can live this out with others, including our in-laws. For example, a young couple is about to purchase their first home. But before they make any decisions about the purchase, the wife's father steps in and begins to tell them where they should buy the home, how much they should spend and why they should buy a house in the suburbs instead of a condo downtown. Now the wife, we will call her Jill, loves her dad and is always open to his suggestions. She thinks that she and her husband (we'll call him Jack) should take Dad's advice. Jack has some concerns about the location and the price and of the house his father-in-law is strongly recommending, but wants Jill to be happy and does not want to upset his father-in-law. In this scenario Jack and Jill have not followed the blueprint for marriage that is laid out in the Bible. When the pair married, Jack was meant to replace Jill's father as the most influential man in her life. Similarly, Jill was meant to replace Jack's mother as the most influential woman in his life. This is how God has seen fit to establish marriage.

Marriage is not about us getting our own way, it is about us following God's will. This leads to the next point some may find contentious, that is, the prevention of women being independent. Paul states in Ephesians 5:23, that Christ is the head of the church, his body, of which He is the Saviour. Collectively as husbands and wives we are the church. Christ is our head and also our Saviour. Being our head cost Christ everything; it cost him his life. He died to save us. We depend on Christ for our salvation. So you see, there is no independence for neither husband nor wife. Both are mutually dependent on God and on each other, but the dependence on their parents will need to change.

We are taking time on this point because many marriages start with the cart before the horse. There is often a sense that independence should be maintained when two people get married. Then both husband and wife are trying to understand why they aren't getting anywhere and why they can't seem to move forward. When women allow their husbands to lead, it is allowing God's plan and purpose to truly be fulfilled. Even if you feel your husband has very poor leadership skills, this is still his role. To take over his role would be to unhook your cart and put it before the horse. Then climb into the cart and expect to go on your journey. It simply won't happen. You will quickly find you are stuck.

Husbands, the privilege to lead your family will require self sacrifice not self-centeredness; because Christ who is leading you must be the purpose for which you lead your family. Again, to take the lead instead of letting Christ do so would be tantamount to unhooking your cart and putting it before the horse yet fully expecting to go somewhere. So how do our parents fit in with all this? Let's take a further look.

Detaching in a healthy way

We have all heard stories about meddling in-laws. Some of you may already be experiencing this situation. As well, there are husbands and wives who dislike his or her spouse's parents. There are of course parents (and siblings) who do not like the decision their loved one has made in his or her choice of spouse. The possibilities are numerous as to how conflict can manifest with respect to in-laws.

With this in mind, it is the newly wed couple's job to set the tone of how these relationships will be managed. We didn't feel in a position to set much of a tone when we were first married, however we discovered later in our marriage that it needed to be done. With this new relationship comes new responsibilities. The couple must lead their respective families in terms of the boundaries around their new marriage. If this does not happen early, often couples find that the boundaries have been set for them by others. Then they begin their new life journey together based on rules that others have established. For instance, if lines are not clearly drawn, parents may feel they still have some control over their child's time, holidays, vacations, financial decisions and much more.

For some couples it can be tempting to allow mom and dad to participate in the decision-making process on issues both big and small. Some newly weds fall back on the safe haven of mom and dad as they nervously navigate all the new responsibilities that come with marriage. While it can be helpful to receive guidance from your parents, as with anything, excess can lead to abuse and imbalance.

Let's look at this example. Dick and Jane need to buy a new car. They have been married two months and this is their first major purchase. They call their parents and ask for advice. Mom and dad give the couple some options to think about but leave the couple to come up with a decision on their own. Mom and dad agree to be in prayer about the decision their children are about to make. This is quite healthy. The Bible tells us that plans fail for lack of counsel (Proverbs 15:22). Dick and Jane benefitted from the wise counsel of their parents, but came to their decision as a couple.

What can become unhealthy is when mom and dad insist on what car to buy, pay for the new car and keep the title in their own names etc, etc. Our in-laws are to be a *re*-source to us. Jesus is to be our source. He is the one we ought to run to with every care both big and small. We need to lean on the Holy Spirit to direct our decisions and seek Him when we are unsure of which way to go. It is the Lord who provides all of our needs.

There will inevitably come times of transition or difficulty where parents will step in to give much needed help. This is wonderful. Couples need this kind of familial support whether it has to do with finances, child care or any of the many issues couples face as they merge two lives.

It is important to honor our parents and in-laws. It may be difficult at times but the Lord requires this from us. If newly married couples always seek to allow the Lord to be their source for guidance, comfort, direction and encouragement, we can allow our parents to be what they are intended to be – a resource. The in-laws' role is to support what the couple has already established.

Chapter *Fifteen*

Parenting

Train a child in the way he should go, and when
he is old he will not turn from it.
Proverbs 22:6

More than likely parenting will not be at the forefront of the minds of newlyweds. While some couples are anxious to get started on their family, others look forward to a few years spending time getting comfortable with each other in married life. Whatever the approach, parenting children is something that a couple should discuss as part of their premarital preparation.

During our courtship I was somewhat ambiguous about whether or not I wanted to have children. This took Robert completely by surprise. He definitely wanted a family. He let me know that not having children would be a deal-breaker for him. He would not be able to continue with the relationship. He was in love and so was I; however our vision for our future needed to line up. I needed to make a decision. After taking time to unpack the motivations I had for remaining childless, I began to see with God's help that these were rooted in fear. I realised that I would actually love to be a mother, all fear aside. Today I can truly say that the love we feel for our children is the identical love we felt for them even before we met them or before they were conceived. Simply the idea of them inspired a deep love.

A common area of tension for newlyweds is unresolved issues around having children. One of the two may still be struggling with the idea of becoming a parent while the other may have a strong desire to have children. This is an issue that should be dealt with early in the courtship phase of a relationship. A couple that chooses to ignore this area of tension will undoubtedly experience challenging times in the months and years to come. Again, asking and answering direct questions openly and honestly now will save you from a lot of pain later. We have provided some suggestions on how you and your partner can start this important conversation. Here are some questions to consider.

Will we have children?

Couples, hide nothing. Be honest and state how you really feel about everything, especially where it involves planning your future family. This is an area that requires open negotiation until a true consensus is reached.

How many will make our family complete?

This is a question that need not necessarily be answered prior to the nuptials, but some consensus should be reached. The Lord impresses on our hearts how our families will take shape. During our engagement we felt strongly that we would have two biological children, but have remained open to God's desire and his heart for our family.

How will we discipline?

Volumes have been written on discipline, but for our purposes we will not be expounding on methods of discipline. Instead, what we hope you will take away from this chapter is that nothing can be assumed. Begin the dialogue now about how you will discipline your children. You need to be in total agreement about the approach you will take with your children. While newlyweds cannot anticipate every situation they will face as parents, the couple must be able to at the very least come up with a philosophy about discipline. For example, some people strongly believe in corporal punishment, while others are vehemently opposed to any kind of physical discipline. It is important that both of you are on the same page about the basic principles of parenting and discipline. It is better to be in agreement now than try to negotiate your position when faced with a tantruming two year old.

What is your vision for your family?

We did not have a clear vision for our family, but rather a general sense of how the Lord was leading us. However, as time has passed our vision has become more defined. This may be the case for you as well. For us, our vision has become to have a Christ-centred marriage in which to raise godly children who will impact their generation to advance the kingdom of God. Whew! That is some vision. But we believe it is really God's vision for marriage and family on a whole. Our families are like little cells that are part of a great body. As part of the body of Christ we have the opportunity to train and disciple little people who will go out into the world and live out Christ's love. Parenting is no small task. It ought to be assumed with a sober sense that it is an awesome privilege and responsibility.

An important point to bear in mind is that you and your partner come from two different families, where the methods of parenting varied. It is vital for each couple to come up with a formula that will work for their family given the temperament and person-ality of each of their children and the parents as well. In doing so, you will find yourself better able to live out God's vision for your family.

Children are a joy and a blessing. They bond a couple very deeply and they provide opportunities to grow us and mature us in many ways. Children are also a source of love, they give it freely and they receive it wholeheartedly. With these truths as a backdrop, we certainly should include them in our marriage plans. Discussions about this area in marriage will be time well spent. The Bible tells us that a function of marriage is to be fruitful and increase in number (Genesis 1:22). In keeping with God's Word, we believe that part of the planning for marriage needs to include planning for parenthood.

Finally, the Bible is the one resource parents can depend on to train their children in the way they should go. It may be true that children don't come with an instruction manual, but we can always count on God's Word to help us guide them in the right direction.

Final Thoughts

This brings us to the end of the Five Factors that will impact your marriage. Taking the time to explore each of these factors will help to produce a lifetime of joy in your marriage. Any journey we take requires careful planning and preparation — and so it is with marriage.

Prepared to be Married

We are thrilled to be finished this project after laboring over it for over four years. Our first five years of marriage were like a child who found himself in the deepest part of the lake trying to make his way back to shore knowing he was growing weaker and weaker as the tide fought against his every stroke. Not only were we fighting against what seemed to be insurmountable pressures, we found ourselves ill equipped for the journey that we had embarked on. Sure we had taken the standard pre-marriage course that was supposed to prepare us for our marriage. However, during our "first five" we found that it did little to extinguish what seemed to be hell on earth, despite its good intentions. So as desperate times called for desperate measures, we did what came naturally; we turned on each other. Just as that child would, upon first contact with his rescuer, we began to panic and fight and do what ever it was that we had to do to preserve our own survival; even at the expense of the other.

We launched a contemptible campaign of a most malicious nature that quickly revealed the true colors that we had both skillfully hidden behind our masks. We began to do things and say things to each other that reflected a heinous hatred not a "richer or poorer" love. It was as though we were two opposing soldiers who had just jumped into the same foxhole. If we were both being forthright, and we are, we both honestly could have walked away from our marriage after only *one* month. But by God's grace and strength, we celebrated our tenth wedding anniversary on June 5th of this year. God has taken us through some battles in our marriage that simply should have been conversations during marriage preparation. But the enduring truth is that He always made sure we came out of the battle on the same side. Our lack of preparation nearly cost us our marriage on several different occasions.

Marriage is like any other endeavor of significance. The more time that you spend preparing, researching, discovering and testing, the better equipped you will be for the journey. Just think for a moment. When a plane is prepared for a flight, there are many people who have spent several hours to ensure that the plane is prepared for one *single* journey. Now think of the preparation that is needed for a life-long journey. The preparation first must begin with the individuals. You must have a strong perception of who *you* are before you join yourself with someone else. Have a firm idea of your motives, expectations, process, outlook and most importantly God's providence when considering a life partner. Then, when that someone comes into your life, don't rush into anything. Take time to *really* get to know that person and let that person *really* get to know you. When you have a solid understanding of who you are, you will be better at discerning who you're compatible with.

In writing this book it was not our intention, nor do we have the credentials, to suggest that we are marriage experts. We are simply a couple who has been given a message to pass back to those who follow us in their own marriage journey. Our efforts are to prepare couples for potential hazards which, we have experienced along our journey, in hopes that they might be avoided. This way, when you cross over the threshold of your new life together, you might experience a little taste of heaven instead of a whole lot of hell.

Appendix
Coupling Questionnaire

"Helping couples come together to stay together"

Motives

- Why do you want to get married?
- Why don't you want to be single?

Expectations

- What expectations do you have about being married?
- What does the ideal marriage look like?
- What don't you want in a marriage?
- What do you think you could bring to a marriage?
- What do you want your partner to bring to your marriage?
- Define your ideal spouse.
- Define what your ideal spouse is not.
- How much of you would you like to see in your partner?

Process

- How would you go about finding your spouse?
- How would you draw this person to you?

Outlook

- What does being married mean to you?
- How much of you do you see in your partner?
- How much does your partner complement you?

Providence

- What sort of legacy have you been left regarding marriage?
- What is God's role in marriage?
- What does God's Word say about marriage?
- What is God's purpose for marriage?
- What is God's role in your current life/relationship?

Notes

Notes

Notes

Notes

Notes

We want to hear from you.
Please visit us online at threefoldministries.com
or contact us at
info@threefoldministries.com

CPSIA information can be obtained at www.ICGtesting.com
Printed in the USA
LVOW102315010812

292553LV00001B/6/P

9 781607 915317